*Funny Letters*
*from*
*Famous People*

# Funny Letters

## from

## Famous People

*Edited by*

CHARLES OSGOOD

BROADWAY BOOKS   NEW YORK

PRINTED IN THE UNITED STATES OF AMERICA

BROADWAY BOOKS and its logo, a letter B bisected on the diagonal, are trademarks of Broadway Books, a division of Random House, Inc.

Visit our website at www.broadwaybooks.com

First edition published 2003

*Book design by Helene Berinsky*

Library of Congress Cataloging-in-Publication Data

Funny letters from famous people / edited by Charles Osgood.— 1st ed.
    p. cm.
      1. Letters.  2. American wit and humor.  I. Osgood, Charles.

PN6131 .F86 2003
826.008'017—dc21                    2002034214

ISBN 0-7679-1175-X

10  9  8  7  6  5  4  3  2  1

*This book is dedicated to*
*Those dauntless men and women who,*
*Sometimes by truck, sometimes by feet,*
*In spite of snow and rain and sleet,*
*And heat of day, and gloom of night,*
*And dogs that bark and sometimes bite,*
*And handwriting that's hard to read,*
*Complete your rounds with all due speed,*
*Brave couriers, hats off to you*
*Who get those funny letters through!*

—CHAS. OSGOOD

# CONTENTS

# INTRODUCTION

Letter writing is close to becoming a lost art in this day of
e-mail, the Internet, word processing, cell phones, and answering machines.

Many people today seldom if ever sit down and write ac-
tual letters anymore. On those rare occasions when they do
try to write a letter, they often find that their letter-writing
skills have atrophied. Besides, they can't find anything decent to write with.

If they find a ballpoint pen, it does not work. Somebody
left the cap off and it dried up. Even if they do find a pen
that works, something to write *on* is also a problem. Writing on a paper bag or the back of a junk-mail ad is considered bad form.

They can't remember where they put the stationery. No
point in looking in the stationery drawer. It was never kept
there. If they do find letter paper, they can't find a proper
envelope.

If they do find a suitable envelope, they can't find the address book. If they do find the address book, it turns out to have only the old address, not the new one. Or, if it does have the current address, it doesn't include the Zip Code.

Even if all the foregoing somehow turn up, something else will be missing; the half-roll of postage stamps that used to be in the middle drawer over the desk. This drawer now contains nothing but old paper clips, thumb tacks, four pennies, the cap that belongs to the dried-up pen, a loose blazer button, etc. etc. No stamps.

In the unlikely event that a stamp of the correct denomination is found (if, indeed, they know what a first-class stamp sells for these days), and they remember what they wanted to say and manage to write it down, and put it in an envelope and address and seal and put a stamp on it, there is still one more crucial step, which is often overlooked.

To get a letter delivered, it is necessary to mail it—i.e., drop it in a U.S. Postal Service mailbox. The stamped, addressed envelope is not going to drop itself into a mailbox. You have to go out in the rain, sleet, gloom of night, or whatever, and do it yourself. If you leave the letter on the kitchen counter, assuming that somebody else in the family will mail it for you, you will find it at least a year later with the stack of old magazines you are throwing out.

All this is very time consuming, and everybody is so busy nowadays watching television that we have neither the patience nor the inclination to go through it. So we don't exchange letters the way people used to, once upon a time when every letter was answered by another, which in turn required a response. This would go on and on for years, decades, lifetimes. And these letters were carefully saved!

These saved letters, preserving thoughts, feelings, and experiences, have been a gold mine for biographers of famous people over the centuries. (Most biographies are about high achievers, aren't they? Why would anyone take all the time and go to all the trouble of researching and writing a big thick book about somebody nobody ever heard of or cares about?)

Where would David McCullough be without all those letters between John and Abigail Adams? Pity the poor biographer two hundred years from now having to rely on the collected e-mail exchanges of George W. and Laura Bush, or of Bill and Hillary Clinton. Not that it wouldn't be interesting, of course. Reading other people's mail is always fascinating. But is e-mail saved anywhere except on your own hard drive and in the secret files of the National Security Agency?

Speaking of the NSA, which eavesdrops on the electronic transmissions of the whole world, we now take it as given that Big Brother has every e-mail ever sent—however frivolous—digitally stored, probably in the same gray government facility at Fort Mead, Maryland, that houses the grapes of wrath. But nobody will ever be allowed to see it. It's written STRICTLY OFF LIMITS to everybody.

As far as e-mail humor is concerned, the only way you

can tell whether anything is supposed to be funny is via the punctuation ☺.

But a real letter about a real situation from a real person, especially a real politician, author, or show business celebrity? Now *that* can be funny!

—CHARLES OSGOOD

# I

# POLITICIANS

*Politics is never far from a politician's mind.*
*And in almost every politician's letter you can find*
*Pointing with pride while at the same time viewing*
         *with alarm,*
*As with wonderful dexterity he almost breaks his arm,*
*Spinning contradictions with such gymnastic knack*
*That with all humility he pats himself upon the back.*
*He often makes us laugh out loud; but what is most*
         *mysterious*
*Is why he's at his funniest when trying to be serious.*

CHARLES OSGOOD

# George Washington

WHEN IT CAME to the subject of marriage, George Washington certainly was of several minds, all of them witty.

A thirty-eight-year-old bachelor, one Tench Tilghman, wrote to General Washington to explain that he had gotten married while on his overstayed leave.

Washington wrote back:

> Dear Tench:
> We have had various conjectures about you. Some thought you were dead, others that you were married.

Washington sent a congratulatory if slightly bizarre message to Governor Henry Lee of Virginia on the occasion of his marriage:

> My dear Gov. Lee:
> You have exchanged the rugged field of Mars for the soft and pleasurable bed of Venus.

About the marriage of his friend Colonel Ward, Washington wrote to a mutual friend:

> I am glad to hear that my old acquaintance Colonel Ward is yet under the influence of vigorous

passions. I will not ascribe the intrepidity of his late enterprise to a mere flash of desires, because in his military career he would have learnt how to distinguish between false alarm and a serious movement. Charity therefore induces me to suppose that like a prudent general, he had reviewed his strength, his arms, and ammunition before he got involved in an action. But if these have been neglected, and he has been precipitated into the measure, let me advise him to make the first onset upon his fair Del Toboso [a reference to the title invented by Don Quixote for his ladylove] with vigor, that the impression may be deep, if it cannot be lasting, or frequently renewed.

# Thomas Jefferson

AT NINETEEN, Thomas Jefferson spent a most unpleasant night sleeping—or trying to sleep—at a friend's house. He wrote to a mutual friend on Christmas Day in 1762, describing his tribulations. The letter, in part:

> The cursed rats ate up my pocketbook which was in my pocket within a foot of my head. And not contented with plenty for the present, they carried away my jemmy-worked silk garters and half a dozen new minuets I had just got.
> Of this I should not have accused the devil—because you know rats will be rats.

Jefferson had a good friend, a Mrs. William S. Smith, who wrote him while he was in Paris to ask him to determine the disposition of some corsets she had ordered there some time before and had yet to receive. Jefferson bought two corsets and sent them to her with a letter explaining that he had no idea whether they would fit, because she had not sent her measurements:

> My dear Mrs. Smith,
> . . . If too small, then lay them aside for a time. There are ebbs as well as flows in this world. When the mountain refused to come to Mahomet, he went to the mountain.

# Abraham Lincoln

ABRAHAM LINCOLN was always prepared to joke about himself—especially when it came to his physical appearance. By the standards of the day, he was indeed considered quite ungainly. He wrote to a friend:

One day . . . I got into a fit of musing in my room and stood resting my elbows on the bureau. Looking into the glass, it struck me what an ugly man I was. The fact grew on me and I made up my mind that I must be the ugliest man in the world. It so maddened me that I resolved, should I ever see an uglier, I would shoot him on sight. Not long after this, Andy [naming a lawyer present] came to town and the first time I saw him I said to myself: "There's the man." I went home, took down my gun, and prowled around the streets waiting for him. He soon came along. "Halt, Andy," said I, pointing the gun at him, "say your prayers, for I am going to shoot you." "Why, Mr. Lincoln, what's the matter? What have I done?" "Well, I made an oath that if I ever saw an uglier man than I am, I'd shoot him on the spot. You are uglier, surely; so make ready to die." "Mr. Lincoln, do you really think that I am uglier than you?" "Yes." "Well, Mr. Lincoln," said Andy deliberately and looking me squarely in the face, "if I am any uglier, fire away."

In a similar vein, Lincoln later wrote to a friend:

> I have one vice, and I can call it nothing else: it is not to be able to say "No." Thank God for not making me a woman, but if He had, I suppose He would have made me just as ugly as He did, and no one would ever have tempted me.

Upon hearing the news in 1841 that his good friend, Joshua F. Speed, had just gotten married, Lincoln offered these words of advice:

> Dear Joshua:
> My old father used to have a saying that "if you make a bad bargain, hug it the tighter"; and it occurs to me that if the bargain you have just closed (marriage) can possibly be called a bad one, it is certainly the most pleasant one for applying that maxim to, which my fancy can, by any effort, picture.
> A. Lincoln

Not surprisingly, at twenty-eight years old, Lincoln was still a bachelor. A friend told him she would bring her sister to

Springfield, Illinois, if Lincoln would consider marrying her. So queried in a confused and embarrassed moment, Lincoln agreed to this plan. The result was disastrous, as Lincoln demonstrates in this wry letter:

. . . Although I had seen her before, she did not look as my imagination had pictured her. I knew she was oversize, but she now appeared a fair match for Falstaff. I knew she was called an "old maid," and I felt no doubt of the truth of at least half of the appellation, but now, when I beheld her, I could not for my life avoid thinking of my mother; and this, not from withered features, for her skin was too full of fat to permit its contracting into wrinkles—but from her want of teeth, weather-beaten appearance in general, and from a kind of notion that ran in my head that nothing could have commenced at the size of infancy and reached her present bulk in less than thirty-five or forty years; and in short I was not at all pleased with her. . . .

But what could I do? I had told her sister that I would take her for better or for worse . . . and was now fairly convinced that no other man on earth would have her, and hence the conviction that they were bent on holding me to my bargain. . . .

At once I determined to consider her my wife, and this done, all my powers of discovery were put to work in search of perfections in her which might be fairly set off against her defects. I tried to imagine her handsome . . . tried to convince myself that the mind was much more to be valued than the person. . . .

After I had delayed the matter as long as I thought I could in honor do (which by the way had brought me round into the last fall) . . . I mustered my resolution and made the proposal to her direct.

But, shocking to relate, she answered No. At first I suppose she did it through an affectation of modesty, which I thought but ill became her under the peculiar circumstances of her case, but on my renewal of the charge I found she repelled it with greater firmness than before. I tried it again and again, but with the same . . . want of success.

And I then . . . for the first time began to suspect that I was really a little in love with her. . . .

I have now come to the conclusion never again to think of marrying, and for this reason—I can never be satisfied with anyone who would be blockhead enough to have me.

A.L.

Strong examples of Lincoln's famous brevity and wit—and stubbornness—are demonstrated in the following exchange of notes between Lincoln and his Secretary of War,

Edwin Stanton. The notes refer to a certain individual whom Lincoln wanted as an army chaplain, but whom Stanton found lacking, and apparently matters ended in a stalemate.

Dear Stanton:
Appoint this man chaplain in the army.
Lincoln

Dear Mr. Lincoln:
He is not a preacher.
E. M. Stanton

Dear Stanton:
He is now.
Lincoln

Dear Mr. Lincoln:
But there is no vacancy.
E. M. Stanton

Dear Stanton:
Appoint him chaplain-at-large.
Lincoln

Dear Mr. Lincoln:
There is no warrant in the law for that.
E. M. Stanton

Dear Stanton:

Appoint him anyhow.

A. Lincoln

Dear Mr. Lincoln:

I will not.

E. M. Stanton

During the Civil War, General George McClellan proved to be more of a hindrance to President Lincoln than a help. He continually pestered Lincoln for more men, more guns, and more horses, and he made each demand seem more urgent than the previous one. Lincoln constantly urged the general to provide more detailed reports of his battles and activities along with his demands for more supplies. This angered McClellan, who then began to focus on trivia. One dispatch read:

President Abraham Lincoln

Washington, D.C.

We have just captured six cows. What shall we do with them?

George B. McClellan

Lincoln immediately dispatched this reply:

George B. McClellan
Army of the Potomac
    As to the six cows captured—milk them.
    A. Lincoln

Lincoln proffered this amusing letter of "recommen-dation" to his friend Judge Stephen T. Logan, in about 1850:

My dear Judge,
    The bearer of this is a young man who thinks he can be a lawyer. Examine him if you want to. I have done so and am satisfied. He's a good deal smarter than he looks to be.

Here's another letter of recommendation, written to Major George D. Ramsey:

October 17, 1861
My dear Sir:
    The lady of this says she has two sons who want to work. Set them at it if possible. Wanting to work is so rare a want that it should be encouraged.
    A. Lincoln

In 1863, a woman wrote Lincoln requesting "a sentiment" along with his autograph. He replied:

Dear Madam:
    When you ask from a stranger that which is of interest only to yourself, always enclose a stamp.
There's your sentiment, and here's your autograph.
    A. Lincoln

# Ulysses S. Grant

A MAN OF WAR who led the Union soldiers to fabled victory against Robert E. Lee and his rebels, our eighteenth president, Ulysses S. Grant, had a famously brusque, blunt style. Here's how he described a battle during the Mexican War in 1847, eighteen years before his most famous victory in the Civil War:

> The Mexicans were giving way all along the line, and many of them, no doubt, left early. There seemed to be a few men in front and I charged upon them with my company. There was no resistance, and we captured a Mexican colonel, who had been wounded, and a few men. Just as I was sending them to the rear with a guard of two or three men, a private came from the front. . . . The ground had been charged over before. My exploit was equal to that of the soldier who boasted that he had cut off the leg of one of his enemy. When asked why he did not cut off his head, he replied, "Someone had done that before."

# Rutherford B. Hayes

IN 1842, Rutherford B. Hayes wrote his mother, a firm believer in temperance, about a cough he had. He told her that the doctors would hold out hope that his life would be prolonged by a dozen years, but only on certain conditions:

Dear Mother—

I will stop drinking, regulate my diet, keep out of the cold, and entirely refrain from laughing.

Several years later, Hayes wrote his sister:

I have had no loves as yet [but] uppermost in the medley of ideas that are rolling about under my hair is that before a year rolls around, I'll get me a wifey, or at least a sweetheart, if I can find one who agrees with me that I am one of the sunniest fellows in the world.

# Benjamin Harrison

MARGARET PELTZ was a close friend of Benjamin Harrison and his family, and in 1877 (eleven years before he was elected president), she sent him some fancy nightshirts. Harrison sent the following grateful note:

Dear Margaret:

... The garments were, I believe, intended for the Governor of Indiana [a tall, gangling man who earned the nickname "Blue Jeans" Williams], but they were too short for him and much too dainty, so I have taken the liberty of keeping them. Mrs. Harrison thought I would not wear ruffled and pleated *robes de nuit* and was surprised to see how kindly I took to the finery. Strange as it may seem, I have never had more *unruffled* sleep.

# *Theodore Roosevelt*

EVER THE ARDENT NATURALIST, Theodore Roosevelt wrote the following to his friend and admirer John Burroughs, who wrote a number of nature books. The letter describes some difficulties in the lives of the bears in Yellowstone Park:

Dear John:

. . . I think that nothing is more amusing and interesting than the development of the changes made in wild beast character by the wholly unprecedented course of things in the Yellowstone Park. There are lots of tin cans in the garbage heaps which the bears muss over, and it has now become fairly common for a bear to get his paw so caught in a tin can that he cannot get it off, and of course great pain and injury follow. Buffalo Jones was sent with another scout to capture, tie up, and cure these bears. He roped two and got the can off one, but the other tore himself loose, can and all, and escaped, owing, as Jones bitterly insists, to the failure of duty on the part of one of his brother scouts, whom he sneers at as "a foreigner." Think of the grizzly bear of the early Rocky Mountain hunters and explorers, and then think of the fact that part of the recognized duties of the scouts in the Yellowstone Park at this moment is to catch this same bear and remove tin cans from the bear's paws in the bear's interest!

T.R.

~~

Roosevelt was truly one of America's most fiercely independent presidents. In this letter to the Department of State, his escalating anger over some fairly minor problems is so vivid that it's actually funny. By the end of it, one might be tempted to tweak Roosevelt by addressing him as "Your Royal Irritance."

Washington, December 2, 1908
To the Department of State:

I wish to find out from the Department why it permitted the Chinese Ambassador today twice to use the phrase "Your Excellency" in addressing the President. Not only law but wise custom and propriety demand that the President shall be addressed only as "Mr. President" or as "the President." It is wholly improper to permit the use of a silly title like "Excellency" (and incidentally if titles were to be allowed at all, this title is entirely unworthy of the position of the President). Any title is silly when given the President. This title is rather unusually silly. But it is not only silly but inexcusable for the State Department, which ought, above all other Departments, to be correct in its usage, to permit foreign representatives to fall into the blunder of using this title. I would like an immediate explanation of why the blunder was permitted and a statement in detail as to what has been done by the Department to prevent the commission of any similar blunder in the future.

Now, as to the address itself. I did not deliver it as handed me because it was fatuous and absurd. I have already had to correct the ridiculous telegram that was drafted for me to send to China on the occasion of the death of the Emperor and the Empress Dowager. I do not object to the utter fatuity of the ordinary addresses made to me by, and by me to, the representatives of foreign governments when they come to me to deliver their credentials or to say good-bye. The occasion is merely formal and the absurd speeches interchanged are simply rather elaborate ways of saying good morning and good-bye. It would of course be better if they were less absurd and if we had a regular form to be used by the Minister and by the President on all such occasions, the form permitting of the slight variations which would be necessary in any particular case. It seems to me that some such form could be devised, just as we use special forms in the absurd and fatuous letters I write to Emperors, Apostolic Kings, Presidents, and the like—those in which I address them as "Great and Good Friend," and sign myself "Your good friend." These letters are meaningless; but perhaps on the whole not otherwise objectionable, when formally and conventionally announcing that I have sent a minister or ambassador or that I have received one. They strike me as absurd and fatuous only when I congratulate the sovereigns on the birth of babies, with eighteen or twenty names, to people of whose very existence I have never heard; or condole with them on the deaths of unknown individuals. Still if trouble would be caused by abandoning this foolish custom, then it would be far more foolish to cause the trouble than it is to keep to the custom.

But, on a serious occasion, as in the present instance where a statesman of rank has come here on a mission which may possess real importance, then there should be some kind of effort to write a speech that shall be simple, and that shall say something, or, if this is deemed inexpedient, that shall at least not be of a fatuity so great that it is humiliating to read it. It should be reasonably grammatical, and should not be wholly meaningless. In the draft of the letter handed me, for instance, I am made to say of the letter I receive: "I accept it with quite exceptional sentiments as a message of especial friendship." Of course any boy in school who wrote a sentence like that would be severely and properly disciplined. The next sentence goes on: "I receive it with the more profound sentiments in that you bring it now no less from the Emperor." What in Heaven's name did the composer of this epistle mean by "more profound sentiments" and "quite exceptional sentiments"? Cannot he write ordinary English? Continuing, at the end of the same sentence he speaks of the new Government and what he anticipates from it, in terms that would not be out of place in a prophecy about Alexander the Great on the occasion of his accession to the throne of Macedon. Politeness is necessary, but gushing and obviously insincere and untruthful compliments merely make both sides ridiculous; and are underbred in addition.

## *Woodrow Wilson*

WOODROW WILSON entertained not even the slightest political inclinations as a young man. Rather, after earning his doctorate at Johns Hopkins University, he embarked on an academic career. At that point, obviously in an exuberant mood, Wilson wrote the following to Ellen Louise Axson, the woman he married a few months later in 1885:

Dear Ellen:

It may shock you—it ought to, but I'm afraid it will not—to learn that I have a reputation amongst most of my kin and certain of my friends for being irrepressible, in select circles, as a maker of grotesque addresses from the precarious elevation of chair seats, as a wearer of all varieties of comic grimaces, as a simulator of sundry unnatural, burlesque styles of voice and speech, as a lover of farces—even as a dancer of the *cancan*!

# Winston Churchill

IN 1919, ENGLAND suffered a severe drought. A prominent British duke, the Duke of Rutland, urged that there be included in the Church of England's prayer book some "Prayers for Rain." Winston Churchill, at that time Secretary of War, heard of this and, signing the letter "Scorpio," penned this satirical missive to the London *Times*:

June 12, 1919
To the Editor of *The Times*
Sir:

Observing reports in various newspapers that prayers are about to be offered up for rain in order that the present serious drought may be terminated, I venture to suggest that great care should be taken in framing the appeal.

On the last occasion when this extreme step was resorted to, the Duke of Rutland took the leading part with so much well-meaning enthusiasm that the resulting downpour was not only sufficient for all immediate needs, but was considerably in excess of what was actually required, with the consequence that the agricultural community had no sooner been delivered from the drought than they were clamouring for a special interposition to relieve them from deluge. Profiting by this experience, we ought surely on this occasion to be extremely careful to state exactly what we want in precise terms, so as to obviate the possibility of any misunderstanding, and to economise so far as possible the need for these special appeals. After so many days of drought, it certainly does not seem unreasonable to ask for a change in the weather, and faith in a favorable response may well be fortified by actuarial probabilities.

While therefore welcoming the suggestion that His Grace should once again come forward, I cannot help feeling that the Board of Agriculture should first of all be consulted. They should draw up a schedule of the exact amount of rainfall required in the interests of this year's harvest in different parts of the country. This schedule could be placarded in the various places of worship at the time when the appeal is made. It would no doubt be unnecessary to read out the whole schedule during the service, so long as it was made clear at the time that this is what we have in our minds, and what we actually want at the present serious juncture.

I feel sure that this would be a much more business-like manner of dealing with the emergency than mere vague appeals for rain. But after all, even this scheme, though greatly favorable to the haphazard methods previously employed, is in itself only a partial makeshift. What we really require to pray for is the general amelioration of the British climate. What is the use of having these piecemeal interpositions—now asking for sunshine, and now for rain? Would it not be far better to ascertain by scientific investigation, conducted under the auspices of a Royal Commission, what is the proportion of sunshine and rain best suited to the ripening of the crops? It would no doubt be necessary that other interests beside agriculture should be represented, but there must be certain broad general reforms in the British weather upon which an overwhelming consensus of opinion could be found. The proper proportion of rain and sunshine during each period of the year; the regulation of the rain largely due to the hours of darkness; the apportionment of rain and sunshine as between different months, with proper reference not only to crops but to holidays; all these could receive due consideration. A really scientific basis of climatic reform would be achieved. These reforms, when duly embodied in an official volume, could be made the object of the sustained appeals of the nation over many years, and embodied in general prayers of a permanent and not of an exceptional character. We should not then be forced from time to time to have recourse to such appeals at particular periods, which, since they are unrelated to any general plan, must run the risk of deranging the whole economy of nature, and involve the interruption and deflection of universal processes, causing reactions of the utmost complexity in many directions which it is impossible for us with our limited knowledge to foresee.

I urge you, Sir, to lend the weight of your powerful organ to the systematisation of our appeals for the reform of the British climate.

Yours very faithfully,

Scorpio

# *Herbert Hoover*

COMMENTING ON HIS earlier days as a surveyor in the High Sierra, Nevada, President Herbert Hoover wrote:

> In these long mountain rides over trails and through the brush, I arrived finally at the conclusion that a horse was one of the original mistakes of creation. I felt he was too high off the ground for convenience and safety on mountain trails. He would have been better if he had been given a dozen legs so that he had the smooth and sure pace of a centipede. Furthermore, he should have had scales as protection against flies, and a larger water tank like a camel. All these gadgets were known to creation prior to the geologic period when the horse was evolved. Why were they not used?

A young visitor to the White House had the unexpected pleasure of being invited to join President Hoover for lunch. Sometime later, Hoover received a note from the boy telling him that no one in the boy's hometown believed he had actually dined with the president, or that spinach had been served. Hoover promptly replied:

The White House

My Dear Stephan:

This is to certify that you lunched at the White House with me. I have never been strong for spinach myself, and I had meant to tell you that you didn't have to eat it.

Herbert Hoover

In response to another child's request for his autograph, Hoover wrote:

I was delighted to see that you were not a professional autograph hunter. Once upon a time, one of those asked me for three autographs. I inquired why. He said, "It takes two of yours to get one of Babe Ruth's."

# *Franklin Delano Roosevelt*

FRANKLIN DELANO ROOSEVELT had quite a close relationship with his mother, to say the least. Here's a letter from Roosevelt to his mother written while on board the *S.S. Carillo* between Cuba and Jamaica in 1912, when he would have been thirty years old:

> We all go about in our shirts, no coats except at meals, but trousers of course. The few women are still entirely covered, but we anticipate what greater heat will bring forth.

In 1935, FDR wrote to his friend and constituent Newton D. Baker in Cleveland:

> Dear Newton:
>
> I was sorry not to have a chance to see you while you were here.
>
> Dan Roper has shown me your letter of September eighteenth. I know you will not mind. I know also that you will not mind my telling you that I think you are entirely wrong in your thought that constitutional amendment will of necessity be an issue in the next presidential campaign.
>
> As a Senator with a sense of humor remarked to

me today, "The Republican National Committee in secret confab searched the woods for an issue; they discarded the constitutional issue and decided in a month or two to come out in favor of the Ten Commandments, proclaiming from housetops that the Democratic Party wished

A.   To amend the Ten Commandments
B.   To add to the Ten Commandments
C.   To scrap the Ten Commandments

On this issue they are confident that they can sweep the country."

I wish much that I could have a chance to see you again. After I get back from my little trip, do run down to Washington and have lunch with me.

In 1937, the U.S. ambassador to England, Robert W. Bingham, wrote to FDR that he would have preferred to wear trousers when he attended the coronation of King George VI, but that all members of the diplomatic corps were requested to wear knee breeches. All the ambassadors had complied, including the Soviet ambassador. FDR wrote back:

Dear Bob:

Having a sense of humor, I have been delighted with your letter in regard to the famous case of Trousers vs. Breeches. My ruling is: that Ambassadors should wear trousers unless the

Sovereign of the State to which he is accredited makes a personal demand for knee breeches. I am fortified in this ruling by the pictures I have seen of Comrade Litvinoff in the aforesaid short pants. If Soviet Russia can stand it, I guess we can too.

Kansan newspaper editor William Allen White was a lifelong Republican who, like many other lifelong Republicans, admired FDR. He once wrote the president asking for a photograph of him in a favorite seersucker suit. Roosevelt sent it to him with a letter which began:

Dear Bill:
Here is the seersucker picture, duly inscribed by the sucker to the seer.

Having read a report that, while on a deer-hunting expedition, Vice President John N. Garner had accidentally shot a cow, FDR wrote the following letter, which was read at a dinner where Garner and his guests planned to enjoy the venison resulting from his hunt.

December 9, 1937
PRIVATE BUT NOT TOO CONFIDENTIAL
Dear Jack:
I have read in the papers that tonight you and twenty-four members of the Senate are attending the funeral of my old friend Bessie. I knew her many

years ago when I was hunting in northern Pennsylvania. She was the pet of the camp and would always come when you whistled and eat out of your hand.

I am sorry, indeed, that Joe Guffey removed the tinkling little bell which was always worn around her neck. It makes me feel so chokey when I think of her untimely demise that I do not think that I could attend the funeral service tonight even if I had been invited.

I understand fully, of course, that this unfortunate hunting accident was not your fault—and I am glad, too, that if Bessie had to go, you shot her instead of whistling her up and cutting her throat with a knife. Dear Bessie probably never knew what hit her.

Under all the unfortunate circumstances attending her death, I hope, nevertheless, that all of you will enjoy the wake.

F.D.R.

FDR ardently believed that women's rights issues deserved wider recognition. But in a letter to his friend Mary Dawson, with tongue firmly implanted in cheek, he expressed his impatience at being "chiseled" by suffragettes:

The White House
Feb. 10, 1949
Dear Molly:

You girls have got to realize that this chiseling
business on your part must stop somewhere. I have
put more girls' faces on postage stamps in the last
seven years than all of my thirty-one predecessors
put together. In fact, old Martha Washington was the
only female face on letters up to my Inauguration. I
even put Whistler's mother on a stamp. And just a
few days ago, Louisa Alcott blossomed forth, even
though she was an awful old prude.

Now, instead of asking me for a special stamp for
the Women's Centennial congress, if you had asked
me to put Greta Garbo's face on a stamp, I might
have listened.

Yes, taking it by and large, a careful survey of the
past seven years shows that you girls, as a matter of
fact, have been so petted and pampered that if any
female voter dares to vote for Dewey, Vandenberg,
or Taft next Fall, you will be out of luck. So,
keep up the good work and if we inaugurate a
Democratic President in 1941, I will guarantee that
he will provide one new female stamp each year.

As ever yours,
Franklin

Roosevelt wrote to his good friend Admiral Ernest J. King to tweak him over his reputation as a fearsome and courageous leader:

The White House
August 12, 1942
Dear Ernie:

You will remember "the sweet young thing" whom I told about Douglas MacArthur rowing his family from Corregidor to Australia—and later told about Shangri-La as the take-off place for the Tokyo bombers.

Well, she came to dinner last night and this time she told *me* something.

She said, "We are going to win this war. The Navy is tough. And the toughest man in the Navy— Admiral King—proves it. He shaves every morning with a blowtorch."

Glad to know you!
As ever yours,
F.D.R.

P.S. I am trying to verify another rumor—that you cut your toenails with a torpedo net cutter.

FDR sent this note to Mrs. Roosevelt in 1942:

Do you remember that about a month ago I got sick of chicken because I got it (between lunch and dinner) at least six times a week? The chicken situation has definitely improved but "they" have substituted sweetbreads, and for the past month I have been getting sweetbreads about six times a week.

I am getting to the point where my stomach positively rebels and this does not help my relations with foreign powers. I bit two of them today.

# Harry Truman

IN A LETTER written to his mother in 1945, shortly after he became president, Harry Truman mock-complained about all the clocks in the White House.

> The ship's clock in Mrs. Wallace's [his mother-in-law] room bangs away in that crazy sailor count of bells. The old grandfather clock in the hall has a high squeaky voice like fat tenors and there is a hoarse clock, a little timekeeper with a big voice—like most small people.

Before he departed to attend the Potsdam Conference in 1945, Truman wrote to his mother:

Dearest mother:

I am getting ready to see Stalin and Churchill and it is a chore. I have to take my tuxedo, tails, preacher coat, high hat, low hat and hard hat.

⌒

Truman was, of course, famous for his "plain speaking." He did not suffer fools lightly, and he found a good deal of his job as president to be a tremendous waste of time. In a letter to his sister in 1947, Truman wrote:

> All the President is, is a glorified public relations man who spends his time flattering, kissing, and

kicking people to get them to do what they are supposed to do anyway.

Truman wrote three whimsical memoranda while at the White House, just before Christmas in 1947:

I have appointed a Secretary of Semantics—a most important post. He is to furnish me 40 to 50 dollar words. Tell me how to say yes and no in the same sentence without a contradiction. He is to tell me the combination of words that will put me against inflation in San Francisco and for it in New York. He is to show me how to keep silent—and say everything. You can very well see how he can save me an immense amount of worry.

Then I have appointed a Secretary of Reaction. I want him to abolish flying machines and tell me how to restore oxcarts, oar boats, and sailing ships. What a load he can take off my mind if he will put the atom back together so it cannot be broken up. What a worry that will abolish for both me and Vyshinsky.

I have appointed a Secretary for Columnists. His duties are to listen to all radio commentators, read all columnists in the newspapers from ivory tower to lowest gossip, coordinate them and give me the result so I can run the United States and the world as it should be. I have several able men in reserve besides the present holder of the job, because I think in a week or two, the present Secretary for

Columnists will need the services of a psychiatrist and will in all probability end up in St. Elizabeth's.

In a note written in November 1949, Truman humorously commented on the formality of dining at the White House, which he frequently referred to as "the finest prison in the world":

Had dinner by myself tonight. Worked in Lee House office until dinnertime. A butler came in very formally and said, "Mr. President, dinner is served." I walk into the dining room in the Blair House. Barnett in tails and white tie pulls out my chair, pushes me up to the table. John in tails and white tie brings me a fruit cup, Barnett takes away the empty cup. John brings me a plate, Barnett brings me a tenderloin. John brings me asparagus, Barnett brings me carrots and beets. I have to eat alone and in silence in the candlelit room. I ring. Barnett takes the plate and butter plates. John comes in with a napkin and silver crumb tray—there are no crumbs but John has to brush them off the table anyway. Barnett brings me a plate with a finger bowl and doily on it. I remove the finger bowl and doily and John puts a glass saucer and a little bowl on the plate. Barnett brings me some chocolate custard. John brings me a demitasse (at home a little cup of coffee—about two good gulps) and my dinner is over. I take a hand bath in the finger bowl and go back to work. What a life!"

When Truman announced his intention to streamline the government severely by getting rid of what he felt were some unnecessary government bureaus, a woman wrote to tell him that she was building a new house and needed furniture. Would he mind sending on a few of the discarded bureaus?

Truman wrote back that he had disposed of the bureaus already, but that if she were interested, he had a "second-hand, no-damned-good cabinet I'd like to get rid of."

Paul Hume's infamous *Washington Post* review of Truman's daughter Margaret's singing performance sent Truman into an infamous rage. Though Hume allowed that Miss Truman was "extremely attractive," he went on to state that she "cannot sing very well" and "has not improved" over the years.

Truman wrote the following letter to the thirty-four-year-old Hume on White House stationery:

Mr. Hume:

I have just read your lousy review of Margaret's concert. I've come to the conclusion that you are an "eight ulcer man on four ulcer pay."

It seems to me that you are a frustrated old man who wishes he could have been successful. When you write such poppy-cock as was in the back section of the paper you work for it shows conclusively that you're off the beam and at least four of your ulcers are at work.

Some day I hope to meet you. When that happens you'll need a new nose, a lot of beefsteak for black eyes, and perhaps a supporter below!

[Westbrook] Pegler [another *Post* columnist], a gutter snipe, is a gentleman alongside you. I hope you'll accept that statement as a worse insult than a reflection on your ancestry.

H.S.T.

# *Adlai Stevenson*

As GOVERNOR OF ILLINOIS, Adlai Stevenson was required to act on numerous bills proposed by the state legislature that he felt did little if anything to represent the best interests of the public. He sent the following letter to veto a bill called "An Act to Provide Protection to Insectivorous Birds by Restraining Cats." It was a golden opportunity for Stevenson to make use of his celebrated dry wit.

To the Honorable Members of the Senate of the Sixty-Sixth General Assembly:

I herewith return, without my approval, Senate Bill No. 93 entitled "An Act to Provide Protection to Insectivorous Birds by Restraining Cats." This is the so-called "Cat Bill." I veto and withhold my approval from this bill for the following reasons:

It would impose fines on owners or keepers who permitted their cats to run at large off their premises. It would permit any person to capture, or call upon the police to pick up and imprison, cats at large. It would permit the use of traps. The bill would have statewide application—on farms, in villages, and in metropolitan centers.

This legislation has been introduced in the past several sessions of the Legislature, and it has, over the years, been the source of much comment—not all of which has been in a serious vein. It may be that the General Assembly has now seen fit to refer it to one who can view it with a fresh outlook. Whatever the reasons for passage at this session, I cannot believe there is a widespread public demand for this law or that it could, as a practical matter, be enforced.

Furthermore, I cannot agree that it should be declared public policy of Illinois that a cat visiting a neighbor's yard or crossing the highway is a public nuisance. It is in the nature of cats to do a certain amount of unescorted roaming. Many live with their owners in apartments or other restricted premises, and I doubt if we want to make their every brief foray an opportunity for a small game hunt by zealous citizens—with traps or otherwise. I am afraid this bill could only create discord, recriminations, and enmity. Also consider the owner's dilemma: To escort a cat abroad on a leash is against the nature of the cat, and to permit it to venture forth for exercise unattended into a night of new dangers is against the nature of the owner. Moreover, cats perform useful service, particularly in rural areas, in combating rodents—work they necessarily perform alone and without regard for property lines.

We are all interested in protecting certain varieties of birds. That cats destroy some birds, I well know, but I believe this legislation would further but little the worthy cause to which its proponents give such unselfish effort. The problem of the cat versus bird is as old as time. If we attempt to resolve it by legislation who knows but what we may be called upon to take sides as well in the age-old problems of dog versus cat, bird versus bird, or even bird versus worm. In my opinion, the State of Illinois and its local governing bodies already have enough to do without trying to control feline delinquency.

For these reasons, and not because I love birds the less or cats the more, I veto and withhold my approval from Senate Bill No. 93.

Respectfully,

Adlai Stevenson, Governor

# Dwight D. Eisenhower

UPON HIS PROMOTION to brigadier general in 1941, Dwight Eisenhower responded to the avalanche of congratulations by writing:

> When they get clear down to my place on the list, they are passing out stars with considerable abandon.

In 1942, Eisenhower wrote a letter to his wife Mamie from dreariest wartime London:

Dear Mamie:
I'm trying to get me a little dog—Scottie by preference. You can't talk war to a dog, and I'd like to have someone or something to talk to, occasionally, that doesn't know what the word means! A dog is my only hope.

Here's an excerpt from a letter to Mamie from Frankfurt in the autumn of 1945:

Dear Mamie:
. . . George Patton has broken in to print again in a big way. That man is going to drive me to drink. He misses more good opportunities to keep his mouth shut than almost anyone I ever knew.

# *John F. Kennedy*

PRESIDENT JOHN F. KENNEDY once received a letter from newspaper columnist Leonard Lyons in which Lyons told him the current prices for signed portrait photos of presidents, past and present: George Washington—$175; Franklin D. Roosevelt—$75; U. S. Grant, $55; John F. Kennedy—$65. Kennedy wrote back immediately:

> Dear Leonard:
>
> I appreciate your letter about the market on Kennedy signatures. It is hard to believe that the going price is so high now. In order not to depress the market any further, I will not sign this letter.

Kennedy had quite a whimsical side. Consider this playful letter to a ten-year-old boy, who had written to ask Kennedy about the "little people" of Irish legend:

> March 1963
> Dear Mark,
>
> I want to thank you for your nice letter. I enjoyed hearing from you and hearing about your school.
>
> Your questions are quite pertinent, coming as they do just before St. Patrick's Day. There are many legends about the "little people," but what they all add up to is this: If you really believe, you will see them.

My "little people" are very small, wear tall black stovepipe hats, green coats and pants, and have long, white beards. They do not have horses. I have never been able to determine where they live. They are most friendly, and their message is that all the peoples of the world should live in peace and friendship.

Since you are interested in the Irish, I want to wish you a happy St. Patrick's Day.

Sincerely,

John F. Kennedy

Barry Goldwater was an excellent photographer. He once took a flattering picture of President Kennedy and sent it to him for an autograph. The picture came back with this inscription:

For Barry Goldwater, whom I urge to follow the career for which he has shown so much talent— photography. From his friend, John Kennedy.

(When, in turn, Goldwater sent Johnson his photograph of him for inscription, Johnson returned it with this inscription, and Goldwater hung it proudly in his chambers:

To Barry Goldwater from his favorite target, Lyndon B. Johnson.)

In his reply to an invitation to attend a testimonial luncheon in honor of Postmaster General Edward Day in Springfield, Illinois, Kennedy didn't pass up the opportunity to tease him:

Dear Edward:

I am delighted to learn of the testimonial luncheon. I know that the Postmaster General will enjoy his day off in Springfield, and I am only sorry that I cannot join in this tribute.

I am sending this message by wire, since I want to be certain that this message reaches you in the right place and at the right time.

# Lyndon B. Johnson

AFTER LADY BIRD JOHNSON had purchased a radio station in Austin, Texas, she spent much time there while Congressman Lyndon Johnson was in Washington. Johnson missed having Lady Bird with him, and on one occasion wrote her the following note:

Dearest Lady Bird:

If you don't start writing me more often, I'm going to have you drafted into the WACS. Then you will have to write to your next of kin at least twice a month.

# *George Bush, Sr.*

HOT ON THE 1988 campaign trail, Michael and Kitty Dukakis got a lot of publicity for their irrepressible public displays of affection. George Bush's campaign staff told him that he and Barbara should try out some PDAs themselves. Bush wrote his wife this note:

8-8-88

Sweetsie:

Please look at how Mike and Kitty do it.

Try to be closer in, more—well er romantic—on camera.

I am practicing the loving look, and the creeping hand.

Yours for better TV and more demonstrable affection.

Your sweetie-pie coo-coo.

Love ya

GB

Bush wrote this letter to a supporter on the subject of his famous aversion to broccoli:

March 27, 1990
Mr. Raymond J. Mitchell
Miami Township, Ohio

Dear Mr. Mitchell:

Barbara was touched by your letter telling her of your wife's rebellion against peas, caused by my rebellion against broccoli.

Tell Janice Ann to "hang in there"; however, Ray, I cannot accept your check even though the cause of which you sent it in is a noble one. I love Baby Ruth's and Heath Bars, too, but I just can't spend your fiver on that. "Eat it today, wear it tomorrow."

Barbara, broccoli lover that she is, joins me in sending our warm best wishes.

Sincerely,

George Bush

Like all celebrities, presidents attract more than their share of unusual people. One group who begged for Bush's attention was an organization of Hawaiian cockroach racers. Bush really went the distance in replying to their letter requesting permission to use his famous phrase—"kinder, gentler"—in a name for one of the racing roaches:

March 27, 1990
Mr. Kimo Wilder McVay
Chairman, Roach Bowl III
Honolulu, Hawaii

Dear Kimo:

I was very pleased to get your letter and to learn that *Kinder Gentleroach* has indeed been officially received as an entry for this year's big race.

I know a lot of thoroughbred roach lovers were disappointed that *Oval Office Roach* did so badly back in 1988, but lots has happened since then.

. . . I am a great believer in the Thousand Points of Light concept, and I salute you and all the others for what you are doing to help battle Multiple Sclerosis.

Please consider this your official permission to permit *Kinder Gentleroach* to enter not only the Roach Bowl classic, but also to run in the Iolani Derby. *Kinder Gentleroach* is willing to submit to an anti-steroid test, saliva test, etc., and I challenge all other roach owners to compel their entries to do the same.

Sincerely,

George Bush

# William Proxmire

LIKE EVERY public official, former Wisconsin Democratic Senator William Proxmire got his share of annoying, even insulting letters. Some of his replies—never mailed, of course, but archived—are hilarious.

One constituent wanted to know why Proxmire voted for the education bill. The constituent wrote:

> Although I am in my early thirties, I am of the old school in believing that the American public can do with less federal aid. We should be made to help ourselves instead of becoming parasites dependent on government "handouts."
>
> In closing, I appreciate receiving a copy of your Congressional Record.

Proxmire replied—or rather, wanted to reply:

> You say you don't want to become a parasite, so I don't think I will send you that copy of the Congressional Record you asked for. You can go out and buy one.

Another constituent offered his views "to serve as a guide in voting."

The Senator wanted to write:

Most of your views are contrary to mine, but I got elected and you didn't. That's the way the old cookie crumbles, pal.

Still another constituent offered the unsolicited opinion that the mere fact that President Eisenhower appointed Earl Warren to the Supreme Court hardly proved that Warren was patriotic.

The reply:

If you are still curious about why Mr. Eisenhower appointed Warren, I suggest you write directly to the farm at Gettysburg. In fact, send all your future letters there. Mr. Eisenhower needs a lot of fertilizer these days, so they say.

# Bob Dole

As ELIZABETH DOLE's fame and power grew over the years, even to the point of being—with her husband—a front-runner for George Bush's choice of a vice president, Bob Dole was utterly undisturbed. When she was appointed Secretary of Transportation, Dole remembered, "There were a lot of stories and a lot of pictures taken. I was always in the picture, but I was never identified. They said, 'The man on the left is the husband.' *People* magazine took an interest in Elizabeth, so a photographer followed us around and took about three hundred pictures. They wound up using three, and one showed us making the bed.

"Some guy out in California whose wife had read the story wrote that he was now helping make the bed. He said, 'Senator, I don't mind your wife getting the job. She's well qualified. She's doing good work. But you've got to stop doing the work around the house. You're causing problems for men all across the country.' "

Dole wrote back:

Buster, you don't know the half of it. The only reason she was helping was because they were taking pictures.

# II

# AUTHORS

*When a writer writes a letter*
*It is likely to be better*
*Than one by someone you can tell*
*Does not put words together well.*
*Authors do that for a living*
*And that's the reason I am giving*
*For putting tellers of good stories*
*Among my letter categories.*
*Authors can be very funny*
*When they're not writing for the money,*
*For the glory or the fame,*
*Or the critical acclaim.*
*I like it when the words they use*
*Are chosen purely to amuse,*
*When they write a funny letter*
*To entertain the letter getter.*

CHARLES OSGOOD

# *Joseph Addison*

BRITISH POET, essayist, and politician Joseph Addison was elected to Parliament in 1708, but is best remembered as a contributor to the *Tatler* and its successor, the *Spectator*. His letters published therein attracted a considerable following in their day, and they have remained popular for their surprising inventiveness and cleverness.

Here's Addison dabbling in a bit of shape-shifting in his "Letter from an Ape":

Madam:

Not having the gift of speech, I have a long time waited in vain for an opportunity of making myself known to you; and having at present the convenience of pen, ink, and paper by me, I gladly take the occasion of giving you my history in writing, which I could not do by word of mouth. You must know, Madam, that about a thousand years ago I was an Indian *brachman*, and versed in all those mysterious secrets which your European philosopher, called Pythagoras, is said to have learned from our fraternity. I had so ingratiated myself by my great skill in the occult sciences with a demon whom I used to converse with, that he promised to grant me whatever I should ask of him. I desired that my soul might pass into the body of a brute creature; but this he told me was not in his power to grant me. I then begged that into whatever creature I should chance to transmigrate, I might still retain my memory, and be conscious that I was the same person who lived in different animals. This he told me was within his power, and accordingly promised on the word of a demon that he would grant me what I desired. From that time forth I lived so unblameably, that I was made president of a college of *brachmans*, an office which I discharged with greater integrity till the day of my death.

I was then shuffled into another human body, and acted my part so very well in it that I became first minister to a prince who reigned upon the banks of the Ganges. I here lived in great honour for several years, but by degrees lost all the innocence of the *brachman*, being obliged to rifle and oppress the people to enrich my sovereign; till at length I became so odious, that my master, to recover his credit with his subjects, shot me through the heart with an arrow, as I was one day addressing myself to him at the head of his army.

Upon my next remove I found myself in the woods under the shape of a jackal, and soon lifted myself in the service of a lion. I used to yelp near his den about midnight, which was his time of rousing and seeking after his prey. He always followed me in the rear, and when I had run down a fat buck, a wild goat, or a hare, after he had feasted plentifully upon it himself, would now and then throw me a bone that was but half picked for my encouragement; but upon my being unsuccessful in two or three chases, he gave me such a confounded gripe in his anger that I died of it.

In my next transmigration I was again set upon two legs, and became an Indian tax-gatherer; but having been guilty of great extravagancies, and being married to an expensive jade of a wife, I ran so cursedly in debt that I durst not show my head. I could no sooner step out of my house, but I was arrested by some body or other that lay in wait for me. As I ventured abroad one night in the dusk of the evening, I was taken up and hurried into a dungeon, where I died a few months after.

My soul then entered into a flying-fish, and in that state led a most melancholy life for the space of six years. Several fishes of prey pursued me when I was in the water, and if I betook myself to my wings, it was ten to one but I had a flock of birds aiming at me. As I was one day flying amidst a fleet of English ships, I observed a huge seagull whetting his bill and hovering just over my head. Upon my dipping into the water to avoid him I fell into the mouth of a monstrous shark that swallowed me down in an instant.

I was some years afterwards, to my great surprise, an eminent banker in Lombard Street; and remembering how I had formerly suffered for want of money, became so very sordid and avaricious that the whole town cried shame of me. I was a miserable little old fellow to look upon, for I had in a manner starved myself, and was nothing but skin and bone when I died.

I was afterwards very much troubled and amazed to find myself dwindled into an emmet. I was heartily concerned to make so insignificant a figure, and did not know but, some time or other, I might be reduced to a mite if I did not mend my manners. I therefore applied myself with great diligence to the offices that were allotted me, and was generally looked upon as the notablest ant in the whole molehill. I was at last picked up, as I was groaning under a burden, by an unlucky cock-sparrow that lived in the neighborhood, and had before made great depredations upon our commonwealth.

I then bettered my condition a little, and lived a whole summer in the shape of a bee; but being tired with the painful and penurious life I had undergone in my last two transmigrations, I fell into the other extreme, and turned drone. As I one day headed a party to plunder a hive, we were received so warmly by the swarm which defended it, that we were most of us left dead upon the spot.

I might tell you of many other transmigrations which I went through, how I was a town rake, and afterwards did penance in a bay gelding for ten years; as also how I was a tailor, a shrimp, and a tom-tit. In the last of these shapes I was shot in the Christmas holidays by a young jacknapes, who would needs try his new gun upon me.

But I shall pass over these and several other stages of life, to remind you of the young beau who made love to you about six years since. You may remember, Madam, how he masked, and danced, and sung, and played a thousand tricks to gain you; and how he was at last carried off by a cold that he got under your window one night in a serenade. I was that unfortunate young fellow, whom you were then so cruel to. Not long after my shifting that unlucky body, I found myself upon a hill in Ethiopia, where I lived in my present grotesque shape, till I was caught by a servant of the English factory, and sent over to Great Britain: I need not inform you how I came into your hands. You see, Madam, this is not the first time that you have had me in a chain; I am, however, very happy in this my captivity, as you often bestow on me those kisses and caresses which I would have given the world for when I was a man. I hope this discovery of my person will not tend to my disadvantage, but that you will still continue your accustomed favours to

Your most devoted humble servant,
PUGG

P.S. I would advise your little shock-dog to keep
out of my way; for as I look upon him to be the most
formidable of my rivals, I may chance one time or
other to give him such a snap as he won't like.

# Charles Lamb

BRITISH ESSAYIST Charles Lamb, who died in 1834, was renowned for his cultivated palate and oenophilia. Having enjoyed an estimable amount of wine at a party, he wrote the following letter of "apology" to his host. It's a wonder that certain passages of this letter haven't found contemporary uses among college students who over-imbibe, the way Andrew Marvell's "To His Coy Mistress" has been so used to seduce reluctant co-eds.

Dear Sir:

It is an observation of a wise man that "moderation is best in all things." I cannot agree with him "in liquor." There is a smoothness and oiliness in wine that makes it go down by a natural channel, which I am positive was made for that descending. Else, why does not wine choke us? Could Nature have made that sloping lane, not to facilitate the downgoing? She does nothing in vain. You know better than I. You know how often she has helped you at a dead lift, and how much better entitled she is to a fee than yourself sometimes, when you carry off the credit. Still there is something due to manners and customs, and I should apologise to you and Mrs. Asbury for being absolutely carried home upon a man's shoulders thro' Silver Street, up Parson's Lane, by the Chapels (which might have taught me better), and then to be deposited like a dead log at Gaffar Westwood's, who it seems does not "insure" against intoxication. Not that the mode of conveyance is objectionable. On the contrary, it is more easy than a one-horse chaise. Ariel in *The Tempest* says

"On a Bat's back do I fly, after sunset merrily."

Now I take it that Ariel must sometimes have stayed out late of nights. Indeed, he pretends that "where the bee sucks, there lurks he," as much as to say that his suction is as innocent as that little innocent (but damnably stinging when he is provok'd) winged creature. But I take it, that Ariel was fond of methaglin, of which the bees are notorious Brewers. But then you will say: What a shocking sight to see a middle-aged gentleman-and-a-half riding upon a Gentleman's back up Parson's Lane at midnight! Exactly the time for that sort of conveyance, when nobody can see him, nobody but Heaven and his own conscience; now Heaven makes fools, and don't expect much from her own creation; and as for conscience, she and I have long since come to a compromise. I have given up false modesty, and she allows me to abate a little of the true. I like to be liked, but I don't care about being respected. I don't respect myself. But, as I was saying, I thought he would have let me down just as we got to Lieutenant Barker's Coal-shed (or emporium), but by a cunning jerk I eased myself, and righted my posture. I protest, I thought myself in a palanquin, and never felt myself so grandly carried. It was a salve under me. There was I, all but my reason. And what is reason? And what is the loss of it? And how often in a day do we do without it, just as well? Reason is only counting, two and two makes four. And if on my passage home, I thought it made five, what matter? Two and two will just make four, as it always did, before I took the finishing glass that did my business. My sister has begged me to write an apology to Mrs. A and you for disgracing your party; now it does seem to me, that I rather honoured your party, for every one that was not drunk (and one or two of the ladies, I am sure, were not) must have been set off greatly in the contrast to me. I was the scapegoat. The soberer they seemed. By the way, is magnesia good on these occasions? . . . But still you will say (or the men and maids at your house will say) that it is not a seemly sight for an old gentleman to go home pick-a-back. Well, may be it is not. But I never studied grace. I take it to be a mere superficial accomplishment. I regard more the internal acquisitions. The great object after supper is to get home, and whether that is obtained in a horizontal posture or perpendicular (as foolish men and apes affect for dignity), I think is little to the purpose. The end is always greater than the means. Here I am, able to compose a sensible rational apology, and what signifies how I got here? I have just sense enough to remember I was very happy last night, and to thank our kind host and hostess, and that's sense enough, I hope.

Charles Lamb


N.B.—What is good for a desperate headache? Why, patience, and a determination not to mind being miserable all day long. And that I have made my mind up to. So, here goes. It is better than not being alive at all, which I might have been, had your man toppled me down at Lieut. Barker's Coal-shed. My sister tends her sober compliments to Mrs. A. She is not much the worse.

Yours truly,

C. Lamb

# Benjamin Franklin

EVER TRYING to resolve awkward or difficult situations, in 1750 Benjamin Franklin wrote this wry "Model of a Letter of Recommendation of a Person You Are Unacquainted With."

Sir,

The bearer of this, who is going to America, presses me to give him a letter of recommendation, though I know nothing of him, not even his name. This may seem extraordinary, but I assure you it is not uncommon here. Sometimes, indeed, one unknown person brings another equally unknown, to recommend him; and sometimes they recommend one another! As to this gentleman, I must refer you to himself for his character and merits, with which he is certainly better acquainted than I can possibly be. I recommend him, however, to those civilities, which every stranger, of whom one knows no harm, has a right to; and I request you will do him all the good offices, and show him all the favor, that, on further acquaintance, you shall find him to deserve. I have the honor to be, etc.

Here's Franklin's letter to the daughter of his close friend Jonathan Shipley. Young Georgiana's pet squirrel,

Mungo, had died, and Franklin wrote to offer some witty comfort:

September 26, 1772

Dear Miss:

    I lament with you most sincerely the unfortunate end of poor Mungo. Few squirrels were better accomplished; for he had had a good education, had traveled far, and seen much of the world. As he had the honour of being, for his virtues, your favorite, he should not go, like common skuggs [a dialect name for a squirrel], without an elegy or an epitaph. Let us give him one in the monumental style and measure, which, being neither prose nor verse, is perhaps the properest for grief; since to use common language would look as if we were not affected, and to make rhymes would seem trifling in sorrow.

*Epitaph*

Alas! Poor MUNGO!

Happy wert thou, hadst thou known

Thy own felicity,

Remote from the fierce bald eagle,

Tyrant of thy native woods,

Thou hadst nought to fear from his piercing talons,

Nor from the murdering gun

Of the thoughtless sportsman.

Safe in thy wired castle,

GRIMALKIN never could annoy thee.
Daily wert thou fed with the choicest viands,
By the fair hand of an indulgent mistress;
But, discontented,
Thou wouldst have more freedom.

Too soon, alas! Didst thou obtain it;
And wandering,
Thou are fallen by the fangs of wanton, cruel RANGER!

Learn hence,
Ye who blindly seek more liberty,
Whether subjects, sons, squirrels, or daughters,
That apparent restraint may be the real protection;
Yielding peace and plenty
With security.

You see, my dear Miss, how much more decent and proper this broken style is, than if we were to say, by way of epitaph,

Here SKUGG
Lies snug,
As a bug
In a rug.

And yet, perhaps, there are people in the world of so little feeling as to think that this would be a good enough epitaph for poor Mungo.

If you wish it, I shall procure another to succeed him; but perhaps you will now choose some other amusement.

Remember me affectionately to all the good family, and believe me ever, Your affectionate friend . . .

Benjamin Franklin

# Washington Irving

THE BURDEN of reciprocal correspondence is more than some can bear, Washington Irving obviously among them. In 1828, he wrote to one Antoinette Bolviller:

Oh! This continually accumulating debt of correspondence! It grows while we sleep, and recurs as fast as we can pay it off. Would that I had the turn and taste for letter-writing of our friend the prince, to whom it seems a perfect delight; who, like an industrious spider, can sit in that little dark room and spin out a web of pleasant fancies from his own brain; or rather, to make a more gracious comparison, like a honey-bee goes humming about the world, and when he has visited every flower, returns buzz–buzz–buzz to his little hive, and works all that he has collected into a perfect honeycomb of a letter. For my part I know no greater delight than to receive letters; but the replying to them is a grievous tax upon my negligent nature. I sometimes think one of the greatest blessings we shall enjoy in heaven will be to receive letters by every post and never be obliged to reply to them. . . .

With the greatest regard, your friend,
Washington Irving

# Gustave Flaubert

A SMITTEN WOMAN named Louise Colet showed a certain persistence in attempting to visit Gustave Flaubert. Apparently, he wasn't interested in letting Mme. Colet down easily. In 1855, he wrote:

Madame:

I was told that you took the trouble to come here to see me three times last evening.

I was not in. And, fearing lest persistence expose you to humiliation, I am bound by the rules of politeness to warn you that *I shall never be in.*

Yours,

G.F.

# Charles Dickens

ENGLISH NOVELIST Charles Dickens usually tried his level best to be polite and considerate under any circumstances, solving tangled social problems of all sorts throughout his rather complicated life. Celebrated illustrator George Cruikshank, whose etchings and drawings grace a number of Dickens's novels to this day, apparently invited himself along to a dinner party. Rather than discourage Cruikshank, Dickens wrote the following prudent and amusing letter to the party's host, W. Harrison Ainsworth:

My Dear Ainsworth,

Cruikshank has been here to say how that he thought your dinner was *last* Saturday, how that he now finds it is *next* Saturday, and how he means to come with me and surprise you. As the surprise, however agreeable, might be too much for Mrs. Touchet, I have thought it best to send you this warning. Mind, you must assume the virtue though you have it not, and feign extravagant astonishment at the sight of the Illustrious George.

Charles Dickens

In 1858, Dickens got his first taste of the writings of George Eliot, who was, unbeknownst to Dickens (and most of the rest of the world), a woman. But he certainly had his suspicions:

Dear Sir:

I have been so strongly affected by the two first tales in the book you have had the kindness to send me through Messrs. Blackwood, that I hope you will excuse my writing to you to express my admiration of their extraordinary merit. The exquisite truth and delicacy, both of the humor and the pathos of the stories, I have never seen the like of; and they have impressed me in a manner that I should find it very difficult to describe to you, if I had the impertinence to try.

In addressing these few words of thankfulness to the creator of the sad fortunes of Mr. Amos Barton, and the sad love-story of Mr. Gilfil, I am (I presume) bound to adopt the name that it pleases that excellent writer to assume. I can suggest no better one; but I should have been strongly disposed, if I had been left to my own devices, to address the said writer as a woman. I have observed what seems to me to be such womanly touches, in those moving fictions, that the assurance on the title-page is insufficient to satisfy me, even now. If they originated with no woman, I believe that no man ever before had the art of making himself, mentally, so like a woman, since the world began. . . .

Dickens wrote this letter to John Bennett, the owner of a clock repair shop:

Gad's Hill Place
Higham by Rochester, Kent
Monday night
Fourteenth September, 1863

My Dear Sir:
   Since my hall clock was sent to your establishment to be cleaned it has gone (as indeed it always has) perfectly well, but has struck the hours with great reluctance, and after enduring internal agonies of a most distressing nature, it has now ceased striking altogether. Though a happy release for the clock, this is not convenient to the household. If you can send down any confidential person with whom the clock can confer, I think it may have something on its works that it would be glad to make a clean breast of.
   Faithfully yours,
   Charles Dickens

# Lady Isabel Burton

LADY ISABEL BURTON, wife of the intrepid explorer/author Sir Richard Burton, often found herself in places and situations that few other women of her station had ever endured. In a letter to her mother in 1865, she described one such situation:

Dear Mother:

It was fortunate that I had the foresight to take iron bedsteads along, as already at Lisbon three-inch cockroaches seethed about the floor of our room. I jumped on to a chair and Burton growled, "I suppose you think you look very pretty standing on that chair and howling at those innocent creatures." My reaction was to stop screaming and reflect that he was right; if I had to live in a country full of such creatures, and worse, I had better pull myself together. I got down among them, and started lashing out with a slipper. In two hours I had a bag full of ninety-seven, and had conquered my queasiness.

# Lewis Carroll

LEWIS CARROLL (Charles Dodgson) was known as a photographer as well as a mathematician; today, of course, he is best known as the author of *Alice's Adventures in Wonderland* and *Through the Looking Glass*.

Here is a hyperbolically apologetic letter that Carroll wrote to a young friend and photographic model, Annie Rogers, in 1867:

My dear Annie:

This is indeed dreadful. You have no idea of the grief I am in while I write, I am obliged to use an umbrella to keep the tears from running down on to the paper. Did you come yesterday to be photographed? And were you very angry? Why wasn't I there? Well the fact was this—I went out for a walk with Bibkins, my dear friend Bibkins—we went many miles from Oxford—fifty—a hundred, say. As we were crossing a field full of sheep, a thought crossed my mind, and I said solemnly, "Dobkins, what o'clock is it?" "Three," said Fipkins, surprised at my manner. Tears ran down my cheeks. "It is the HOUR," I said. "Tell me, tell me, Hopkins, what day is it?" "Why, Monday, of course," said Lupkins. "Then it is the DAY!" I groaned. I wept. I screamed. The sheep crowded round me, and rubbed their affectionate noses against mine. "Mopkins!" I said. "You are my oldest friend. Do not deceive me, Nupkins! What year is this?" "Well, I *think* it's 1867," said Pipkins. "Then it's the YEAR!" I screamed, so loud that Tapkins fainted. It was all over: I was brought home, in a cart, attended by faithful Wopkins, in several pieces.

When I have recovered a little from the shock, and have been to the seaside for a few months, I will call and arrange another day for photographing. I am too weak to write this myself, so Zupkins is writing it for me.

Your miserable friend,
Lewis Carroll

# Oliver Wendell Holmes, Sr.

AUTHOR, PHYSICIAN, and father of the famous twentieth-century jurist Oliver Wendell Holmes, Sr., was clear about matters for which he had a healthy dislike, as this highly specific letter to the Reverend James Freeman Clarke amply and humorously demonstrates:

October 24, 1862

My dear James,

I received your circular for a meeting of the "Protective War-Claim Association" last week, and now I have a new one, which I feel bound to answer.

I go very little to society and club meetings. Some feel more of a call that way, others less; I among the least.

I hate the calling of meetings to order. I hate the nomination of officers, always fearing lest I should be appointed secretary. I hate being placed on committees. They are always having meetings at which half are absent and the rest late. I hate being officially and necessarily in the presence of men most of whom, either from excessive zeal in the good cause or from constitutional obtuseness, are incapable of being *bored*, which state is to me the most exhausting of all conditions, absorbing more of my life than any kind of active exertion I am capable of performing.

I am slow in apprehending parliamentary rules and usages, averse to the business details many persons revel in; and I am not in love with most of the actively stirring people whom one is apt to meet in all associations for doing good.

Some trees grow very tall and straight and large in the forest close to each other, but some must stand by themselves or they won't grow at all. . . . I have [long] recognized an inaptitude, not to say ineptitude, belonging to me in connection with all such proceedings.

"What if everybody talked in this way?" The Lord arranges his averages in such a way that to every one person like myself there are two or three organizing, contriving, socializing intelligences, and three or four self-sacrificing people, who have forgotten what they like and what they hate by nature, and about a dozen good indifferent folks that will take part in anything they are asked to.

# Horace Greeley

THE FAMED nineteenth-century journalist Horace Greeley was beset by financial woes for many years. While he was editor of the *New York Tribune*, which he funded, he received many begging letters. Here's a typical example:

Dear Sir:

In your extensive correspondence you have undoubtedly secured several autographs of the late distinguished American poet, Edgar A. Poe. If so, will you please favor me with one, and oblige.

Yours respectfully,

A.B.

Greeley shot off the following response:

Dear Sir:

I happen to have in my possession but one autograph of the late distinguished American poet Edgar A. Poe. It consists of an I.O.U., with my name on the back of it. It cost me just $51.50, and you can have it for half price.

Yours,

Horace Greeley

# Mark Twain

SAMUEL L. CLEMENS (better known as Mark Twain) penned this drolly disgruntled letter of complaint to the gas and electric company in Hartford, Connecticut. Twain suffered the incompetence of others with hilarious aplomb. This letter, by the way, was never mailed.

Gentlemen,

There are but two places in our whole street where lights could be of any value, by any accident, and you have measured and appointed your intervals so ingeniously as to leave each of those places in the centre of a couple of hundred yards of solid darkness. When I noticed that you were setting one of your lights in such a way that I could almost see how to get into my gate at night, I suspected that it was a piece of carelessness on the part of the workmen, and would be corrected as soon as you should go around inspecting and find it out. My judgment was right; it is always right, when you are concerned. For fifteen years, in spite of my prayers and tears, you persistently kept a gas lamp exactly half way between my gates; and then furnished such execrable gas that I had to hang a danger signal on the lamp post to keep teams from running into it, nights. Now I suppose your present idea is to leave us a little more in the dark.

Don't mind us—out our way; we possess but one

vote apiece, and no rights which you are in any way bound to respect. Please take your electric light and go to—but never mind, it is not for me to suggest; you will probably find the way; and anyway you can reasonably count on divine assistance if you lose your bearings.

S. L. Clemens

But here's a letter Twain *did* send to the local gas company in Hartford when, in the middle of winter, they shut off his service without any notification:

February 12, 1891

Dear Sirs:

Some day you will move me almost to the verge of irritation by your chuckle-headed Goddamned fashion of shutting your Goddamned gas off without giving any notice to your Goddamned parishioners. Several times you have come within an ace of smothering half of this household in their beds and blowing up the other half by this idiotic, not to say criminal, custom of yours. And it has happened again to-day. Haven't you a telephone?

Ys

S. L. Clemens

At the height of his career, Twain received a request from the director of a theater company who wanted to dramatize *Tom Sawyer*. The director requested Clemens's permission to use the name "Mark Twain" in announcing the production and concluded his letter by offering the author a free ticket to the performance.

Clemens replied with scathing wit, although again he never actually mailed the letter:

Hartford

September 8, '87

Dear Sir,

And so it has got around to you, at last; and you also have "taken the liberty." You are No. 1365. When 1364 sweeter and better people, including the author, have tried to dramatize *Tom Sawyer* and did not arrive, what sort of show do you suppose you stand? That is a book, dear Sir, which cannot be dramatized. One might as well try to dramatize any other hymn. *Tom Sawyer* is simply a hymn, put into prose form to give it a worldly air. . . .

. . . I have seen Tom Sawyer's remains in all the different kinds of dramatic shrouds there are. You cannot start anything fresh. Are you serious when you propose to pay my expence—if that is the Susquehannian way of spelling it? And can you be aware that I charge a hundred dollars a mile when I travel for pleasure. Do you realize that it is 432 miles to Susquehanna? Would it be handy for you to send me the $43,200 first, so I could be counting it as I come along; because railroading is pretty dreary to a sensitive nature when there's nothing sordid to buck at for Zeitvertreib.

Now as I understand it, dear and magnanimous 1365, you are going to recreate *Tom Sawyer* dramatically, and then do me the compliment to put me in the bills as father of this shady offspring? Sir, do you know that this kind of compliment has destroyed people before now? Listen.

Twenty-four years ago, I was strangely handsome. The remains of it are still visible through the rifts of time. I was so handsome that human activities ceased as if spellbound when I came in view, and even inanimate objects stopped to look—like locomotives, and district messenger boys and so-on. In San Francisco, in rainy season I was often mistaken for fair weather. Upon one occasion I was traveling in the Sonora region, and stopped for an hour's nooning, to rest my horse and myself. All the town came out for a look. A Piute squaw named her baby after me,—a voluntary compliment which pleased me greatly.

Other attentions were paid me. Last of all arrived the president and faculty of Sonora University and offered me the post of Professor of Moral Culture and Dogmatic Humanities; which I accepted gratefully, and entered at once upon my duties. But my name had pleased the Indians, and in the deadly kindness of their hearts they went on naming their babies after me. I tried to stop it, but the Indians could not understand why I should object to so manifest a compliment. The thing grew and grew and spread and spread and became exceedingly embarrassing. The University stood it a couple of years; but then for the sake of the college they felt obliged to call a halt, although I had the sympathy of the whole faculty.

The president himself said to me, "I am sorry as I can be for you, and would still hold out if there were any hope ahead; but you see how it is: there are a hundred and thirty-two of them already, and fourteen precincts to hear from. The circumstance has brought your name into most wide and unfortunate renown. It causes much comment—I believe that is not an overstatement. Some of this comment is palliative, but some of it— by patrons at a distance, who only know the statistics without the explanation,—is offensive, and in some cases even violent. Nine students have been called home. The trustees of the college have been growing more and more uneasy all these last months—steadily along with the implacable increase in your census—and I will not conceal from you that more than once they have touched upon the expediency of a change in the Professorship of Moral Culture. The coarsely sarcastic editorial in yesterday's Alta,—headed Give the Moral Acrobat a Rest—has brought things to a crisis, and I am charged with the unpleasant duty of receiving your resignation."

I know you only mean me a kindness, dear 1365, but it is a most deadly mistake. Please do not name your Injun for me.

Truly yours,
S. L. Clemens

⌐⌐

In 1900, when Twain lived on West Tenth Street in Manhattan, he had occasion to write the following letter to a neighbor there:

Dear Madam,

I know I ought to respect my duty and perform it, but I am weak and faithless where boys are concerned, and I can't help secretly approving pretty bad and noisy ones, though I do object to the kind that ring doorbells. My family try to get me to stop the boys from holding conventions on the front steps, but I basely shirk out of it because I think the boys enjoy it.

My wife has been complaining to me this evening about the boys on the front steps and under compulsion I have made some promises. But I am very forgetful, now that I am old, and my sense of duty is getting spongy.

Very truly yours,

S. L. Clemens

# William Dean Howells and Mark Twain

TWAIN AND AUTHOR William Dean Howells were longtime friends. When Twain invited Howells and several other friends to join "The Modest Club," of which he was founder—and sole member—Twain got this reply from Howells:

My dear Clemens:

The only reason I have for not joining the Modest Club is that I am too modest: that is, I am afraid that I am not modest enough. If I could ever get over this difficulty, I should like to join, for I approve highly of the club and its objects: it is calculated to do a great deal of good, and it ought to be given an annual dinner at the public expense. If *you* think I am not too modest, you may put my name down, and I will try to think the same of you. Mrs. Howells applauded the notion of the Club from the very first. She said that she knew *one* thing: that *she* was modest enough, *any*way. Her manner of saying it implied that the other persons you had named were not, and created a painful impression in my mind. I have sent your letter and the rules to Hay. But I doubt his modesty; he will think he has a *right* to belong as much as you or I. . . .

When Howells was nearly felled by scarlet fever in 1884, Twain wrote his friend the following:

My dear Howells,

"O my goodn's" as Jean says. You have now encountered at last the heaviest calamity that can befall an author. The scarlet fever, once domesticated, is a permanent member of the family. Money may desert you, friends forsake you, enemies grow indifferent to you, but the scarlet fever will be true to you, through thick and thin, till you be all saved or damned, down to the last one. I say these things to cheer you. . . . You folks have our most sincere sympathy.

In 1907, Twain sent the following to Howells, at that time considered a leading man of letters in America.

To the Editor,

Sir to you, I would like to know what kind of a goddam govment this is that discriminates between two economic carriers & makes a goddam railroad charge everybody equal & lets a goddam man charge any goddam price he wants to for his goddam opera box.

W. D. Howells

Tuxedo Park Oct. 4

(goddam it)

Howells, it is an outrage the way the govment is acting so I sent this complaint to the N.Y. Times with your name signed because it would have more weight.

Mark

## Oscar Wilde and James Abbott McNeill Whistler

IT COULD BE SAID that both Oscar Wilde and James Abbott McNeill Whistler hoisted egomania to an art form. In 1883, when *Punch* magazine described them as gossiping in public about Sarah Bernhardt, Wilde fired off this telegram to Whistler:

> *Punch* too ridiculous. When you and I are together, we never talk about anything but ourselves.

Whistler cabled back later that day:

> No, no Oscar, you forget. When you and I are together, we never talk about anything except me.

# Oscar Wilde

IN THE DIFFICULT LAST YEAR of his convoluted life, Wilde wrote the following letter to his friend Frances Forbes-Robertson:

My dear, sweet, beautiful friend,

Eric has just sent me your charming letter, and I am delighted to have a chance of sending you my congratulations on your marriage, and all the good wishes of one who has always loved and admired you. I met Eric by chance, and he told me he had been over to the marriage. He was as picturesque and sweet as usual, but more than usually vague. I was quite furious with him. He could not quite remember who it was you had married, or whether he was fair or dark, young or old, tall or small. He could not remember where you were married, or what you wore, or whether you looked more than usually beautiful. He said there were a great many people at the wedding, but could not remember their names. He remembered, however, Johnston being present. He spoke of the whole thing as a sort of landscape in a morning mist. Your husband's name he could not for the moment recall: but said he thought he had it written down at home. He went dreamily away down the Boulevard followed by violent reproaches from me, but they were no more to him than the sound of flutes: he wore the sweet smile of those who are always looking for the moon at midday.

So, dear Frankie, you are married, and your husband is a "king of men"! That is as it should be: those who wed the daughters of the gods are kings, or become so. . . . Like dear St. Francis of Assisi I am wedded to Poverty: but in my case the marriage is not a success: I hate the Bride that has been given to me: I see no beauty in her hunger and her rags. I have not the soul of St. Francis: my thirst is for the beauty of life: my desire is for its joy. But it was dear of you to ask me [to come and visit], and do tell the "king of men" how touched and grateful I am by the invitation you and he have sent me.

And, also, sometime send me a line to tell me of the beauty you have found in life. I live now on echoes, as I have little music of my own.

Your old friend,
Oscar

# Editors

MASTERPIECES AREN'T always appreciated from the outset. After examining *Remembrance of Things Past*, an editor at Ollendorf wrote Marcel Proust:

> My dear fellow,
>     I may perhaps be dead from the neck up, but rack my brains as I may I can't see why a chap should need thirty pages to describe how he turns over in bed before going to sleep.

For that matter, one Herbert R. Mayes, editor of the old *Pictorial Review*, turned down what would have been one of the hottest serializations of the decade: a prepublication offer to serialize Margaret Mitchell's *Gone With the Wind*. He wrote to Mitchell's publisher in 1936:

> A period novel! About the Civil War! Who needs the Civil War now—who cares?

# Sherwood Anderson

OBVIOUSLY LESS than enchanted with his work situation, Sherwood Anderson wrote this letter to his employer, Bayard Barton, in 1918:

Dear Barton:

You have a man in your employ that I have thought for a long time should be fired. I refer to Sherwood Anderson. He is a fellow of a good deal of ability but for a long time I have been convinced that his heart is not in his work. There is no question but that this man Anderson has in some ways been an ornament to our organization. His hair, for one thing, being long and mussy gives an artistic carelessness to his personal appearance that somewhat impresses such men as Frank Lloyd Wright and Mr. Curtiniez of Kalamazoo when they come into the office. But Anderson is not really productive, as I have said, his heart is not in his work. I think he should be fired, and if you will not do the job, I should like permission to fire him myself. I, therefore, suggest that Anderson be asked to sever his connections with the company [on the first of next week]. He is a nice fellow. We will let him down easy, but let's can him.

Respectfully submitted,
Sherwood Anderson

# James Joyce

WE OFTEN FORGET that the enigmatic James Joyce was also quite witty. In his reply to a letter from Harriet Shaw Weaver, Joyce humorously described at length some of the conflicting myths which surrounded him.

71 rue du Cardinal Lemoine
Paris V
24 June 1921
Dear Miss Weaver:

. . . A nice collection could be made of legends about me. Here are some. My family in Dublin believe that I enriched myself in Switzerland during the war by espionage work for one or both combatants. Triestines, seeing me emerge from my relative's house occupied by my furniture for about twenty minutes every day and walk to the same point, the G.P.O., and back (I was writing *Nausikaa* and *The Oxen of the Sun* [for *Ulysses*] in a dreadful atmosphere) circulated the rumour, now firmly believed, that I am a cocaine victim. The general rumour in Dublin was (till the prospectus of *Ulysses* stopped it) that I could write no more, had broken down, and was dying in New York. A man from Liverpool told me he had heard that I was the owner of several cinema theatres all over

Switzerland. In America there appear to be or have been two versions: one that I was an austere mixture of the Dalai Lama and sir Rabindranath Tagore. Mr. Pound described me as a dour Aberdeen minister. Mr. Lewis [Wyndham Lewis] told me he was told that I was a crazy fellow who always carried four watches and rarely spoke except to ask my neighbor what o'clock it was. Mr. Yeats seemed to have described me to Mr. Pound as a kind of Dick Swiveller. What the numerous (and useless) people to whom I have been introduced here think I don't know. My habit of addressing people I have just met for the first time as "Monsieur" earned for me the reputation of a *tout petit bourgeois* while others consider what I intend for politeness as most offensive. . . . One woman here originated the rumour that I am extremely lazy and will never do or finish anything. (I calculate that I must have spent nearly 20,000 hours in writing *Ulysses*.) A batch of people in Zurich persuaded themselves that I was gradually going mad and actually endeavoured to induce me to enter a sanitorium where a certain Doctor Jung (the Swiss Tweedledum who is not to be confused with the Viennese Twiddledee, Dr. Freud) amuses himself at the expense (in every sense of the word) of ladies and gentlemen who are troubled with bees in their bonnets.

I mention all these views not to speak about myself but to show you how conflicting they all are. The truth probably is that I am a quite commonplace person undeserving of so much imaginative painting. . . .

# George Bernard Shaw

GEORGE BERNARD SHAW was as prolific a letter writer as he was a playwright, essayist, and critic. Here Shaw describes "a most fearful tragedy" to his friend Janet Achurch:

29 Fitzroy Square W.
14th January 1896
Dear Janet:

. . . A most fearful tragedy has happened to me. It is impossible that I should see you for a month at least; so all idea of your coming back to town or my going down to St. Leonards must be abandoned. Today I went to get my hair cut. The man asked whether I wanted it short. I said "Yes," and was about to add certain reservations when he suddenly produced an instrument like a lawnmower. All in an instant my golden locks fell like withered grass to the floor and left my head like the back of a Japanese pug dog. Nothing escaped except a little wiglike oasis on the top. I say wiglike; for the climax of the horror was that, unknown to me, these auburn tresses with which you are familiar, concealed a grey—nay, a *white*—undergrowth, which is now an overgrowth. People ask me now what fearful shock I have experienced to turn my hair white in a single night. There must be some frightful mistake about my age:

I am not in my fortieth year, but in my sixtieth. For God's sake, tell me that you believe that it will grow red again—at least that you hope so. . . .

G.B.S.

<hr />

Indeed, Shaw was well known as a wag. He CABLED the following invitation to Sir Winston Churchill:

Have reserved two tickets for my first night. Come and bring a friend, if you have one.

G Shaw

But Churchill was certainly no less witty. His reply:

Impossible to come first night. Will come second night, if you have one.

Churchill

<hr />

After a speaking engagement at Magdalen College at Oxford University in 1892, Shaw wrote the following letter to the editor of the *Pall Mall Gazette*. A man of strong opinions and a nearly lifelong socialist, Shaw was a controversial figure, an image he fostered. At the time of his lecture, he was labeled by many a "revolutionist," and a large group of Oxford students vigorously objected to his very appearance at the university. Once the lecture was under way, that group actually locked the doors of the filled lecture hall and then banded together in an adjoining room, where they tried to drown out Shaw's speech with their own racket. Here, with withering sarcasm, Shaw wittily describes the lengths to which those students went to declare their objections.

Occurred on Saturday, February 20th, 1892, at Oxford
"Revolutionary Progress at Oxford"

Sir,

Will you be so good as to allow me to use your columns to thank the members of Magdalen College, Oxford, for the very enthusiastic welcome which they have just accorded to the first Socialist who has ever lectured within their walls?

The greatest difficulty with which a public speaker has to struggle is the tendency of the audience to leave before the close of his remarks. I therefore desire especially to thank the thoughtful and self-sacrificing body of undergraduates who voluntarily suffered exclusion from the room in order that they might secure the door on the outside and so retain my audience screwbound to the last syllable of the vote of thanks. I desire to explain, however, that I do not advocate the indiscriminate destruction of property as a first step towards Socialism, and that their action in entirely wrecking the adjoining chamber by a vigorous bombardment of coals, buckets of water and asafoetida, though well meant, was not precisely on the lines which I was laying down inside. Nor, though I expressed myself as in favor of a considerable extension of Communism in the future, did I contemplate the immediate throwing of all the portable property in the lobby into a common stock, beginning with my own hat, gloves, and umbrella. Not that I grudge these articles to Magdalen College, but that I wish them to be regarded as an involuntary donation from myself to the present holders rather than as having been scientifically communized.

Speaking as a musical critic, I cannot say that the singing of the National Anthem which accompanied these modest beginnings of revolution was as sincere as that of Ta-ra-ra-boom-de-ay, which one of my friends within the room loudly supported at the general request by a pianoforte accompaniment. It is injurious to the voice, I may add, to sing in an atmosphere rendered somewhat pungent by the projection of red pepper on a heated shovel.

I need not dwell on the friendly care which was taken not to unscrew the door until our proceedings were entirely over. I wish to say, however, that we should not have incommoded our friends by crowding the staircase had not the rope formed of two blankets, by which we were originally intended to proceed from the apartment directly into the open air, unhappily giving way under the strain of being energetically steadied at one end by the outside and at the other by the inside party. There was really no chance of the friction igniting the blankets; so that the pains of the attack posted at an upper window to keep them drenched with water was unnecessary. The gentleman who rendered me a similar attention from the landing above as I descended the stairs also wasted most of his moisture through infirmity of aim; but his hospitable desire to speed the parting guest was unmistakable.

Although my admirers mustered in such numbers that there were at least three times as many persons outside the door as inside (including a don), I am credibly assured that if I had lectured in Brasenose my reception would have been still more overwhelming, and I quite believe it. I was the more overcome as I visited Magdalen under the impression that I was to pass a quiet hour chatting with a few friends and had no idea until I arrived that I was expected to address a meeting or that my advent had roused so deep an interest.

George Bernard Shaw

# William Dean Howells

AMERICAN AUTHOR William Dean Howells wrote this to one Sarah Orne Jewett in 1901:

> My Dear Miss Jewett:
>
> I am almost wounded more by your supposition that I could let anything in the way of work keep me from answering you than I am by the fact that *I never got your letter.*
>
> I am going home with an arrow in my breast that sticks through the back of my coat in a way that will excite universal comment. But I hope to pull it before next summer, and we all hope to see you, for we expect to be back next summer, for York has done Mrs. Howells good. She joins Pilla and me in lasting affection to you and yours.
>
> Sincerely Yours,
> W. D. Howells

Howells certainly waxed rhapsodic when he tendered his regrets to a Lilla C. Perry in 1913:

> Dear Mrs. Perry:
>
> Impossible—impossible! The shattered prose of my being could never rise to the poetry of your most hospitable, most lovable wish to have me as your

guest! I must stay where I can be shy and glum
when I will, or want. . . . But I thank you, I
thank you.

Yours Sincerely,

W. D. Howells

# H. L. Mencken

H. L. MENCKEN sent his good friend Theodore Dreiser the following letter, teasing him about the fact that Mencken hadn't heard from him in a very long time:

*The Theodore Dreiser's Widows and Orphans*
*Relief and Aid Association.*
Rev. Henry Van Dyke, Secy.
Stuart P. Sherman, Treas.

Los Angeles
September 26, 1921

Dear Mr. Mencken:

Your letter of inquiry in regard to the last resting place of the late Theodore Dreiser has been referred to us. Mr. Dreiser died without visible means of support of any kind and his body now lies in row eight, grave number seventeen of the present L.A. Gas Works extension of what was recently the old St. Ignaz Cemetery. Unless his remains are removed and properly marked within the next ten months they are in danger of being completely obliterated.

In accordance with his request at the time of his death the pine board which was placed at his head was only marked with the cryptic numerals *181*. There has been much speculation as to the exact meaning of these. Prof. Silas Carriagewasher of Alfalfa University and long a friend of the late author is of the opinion that they relate to the ancient Coptic [here Mencken drew and underlined three symbols] of which language Mr. Dreiser was a profound student and are equivalent to "the angels." Freely interpreted, Prof. Carriagewalker explains, these might humorously refer to the modern phrase "gone to join the angels," although he adds that such may not have been his intention.

However, since your letter indicates an intention to contribute a floral offering of some kind we suggest that in view of the many unsettled obligations of the author and his numerous widows and dependents that you make your testimonial, however slight, in cash. As far as at present Mr. Dreiser left seventy-nine widows and three hundred and fifteen children, all destitute. These need to be looked after in some way and in consequence a sub-committee of the Southern California Authors' League has been appointed to gather such means as it can. Thus far seven dollars and eighty-three cents have been acquired but the sub-committee is in hopes that more will be forthcoming shortly. Anything that you have to offer will be gratefully received. All sums contributed are immediately divided pro rata, each child and widow counting as one.

Respy.,

The Theodore Dreiser's Widows and Orphans Relief and Aid Association.

Per Henry Van Dyke, Sec'y

Stuart P. Sherman, Treas.

Here's another waggish letter from Mencken to Dreiser:

Dear Sir:

Mr. Mencken requests me to inform you that he is quite ignorant of the matters to which you refer. He further instructs me to ask you to kindly refrain from pestering him with a long and vain correspondence. He is engaged at the moment upon patriotic work which takes his whole time, and he has no leisure to fool with the bughousery of the literati.

Having no more to say, I will now close.

Very sincerely yours,

Ferdinand Balderdash

Captain, 16th U.S. Secret Service

# Carl Sandburg

In 1918, Sam T. Hughes, the editor-in-chief of the News-paper Enterprise Association, wanted to send poet Carl Sandburg (then a journalist) to Stockholm to become a European correspondent. Difficulties arose when the pass-port officers wanted to know precisely why Sandburg had been selected for this position. Sandburg sent Hughes the following letter, which gives his answer to the officers' question:

> Chicago
> July 23, 1918
> Dear Sam:
>
> Passport authorities want a statement from you why [you're sending] me to Stockholm. Recite for them that I am 40 years of age, was born in Galesburg, Ill., and have lived all my life in the United States, except the time for an expedition to Porto Rico in 1898 as an enlisted soldier with the Sixth Illinois volunteers, that I am a newspaper man and for the past six years have been continuously in active newspaper work in Chicago: that I am leaving a position as editorial writer on the Chicago *Daily News*, the world's largest afternoon newspaper, to go to Stockholm for the Newspaper Enterprise Association, which serves [320] newspapers with

news stories and descriptive articles and has a circulation going to 4,500,000 subscribers, being the most extensive service of its kind in the world. Tell them I have cooperated actively with the American Alliance for Labor and Democracy, which is the loyalty legion of the American Federation of Labor, and that the alliance gave wide circulation to my war poem, "The Four Brothers." Make me important as hell. Make it look as though there ought to be brass bands and girls in white dresses strewing flowers on my pathway to the steamboat slip.

. . . I go to Galesburg, Ill., this afternoon to get my mother to swear I was born when I was. They might take a week by mail, for such an affidavit. In Thursday's morning mail I expect your statement which with birth affidavit, will go forward with application for passport. The passport will then be mailed to any point I designate. . . .

I figure on leaving the *Daily News* Wednesday of next week. Mr. [Charles] Dennis, the managing editor, said I was "specially fitted for the Stockholm post" and Julian Mason of the *Evening Post* was tickled. It seems to me I've got to hunt up some sort of live copy and stories or some good friends will be sore. My hunch is that I will find several Big Stories.

This letter is terribly personal. But so is getting a passport. They want to know every mole and scar on a guy's frame. And he has to go get mugged and hand in three pictures of what kind of a pickpocket he looks like.

Sincerely,

C.S.

⌒

Sandburg wrote the following letter, in 1927, to the editor of *Century Magazine* about some articles they had published on his folk-singing concerts.

To the Editor:—

Would you kindly correct the statement published a number of times that in the song-offering in my recital-concerts I employ a banjo?

The instrument used is one with less repercussion, and more intimations of silence, than a banjo.

Sometimes when the strings of it are thrummed one has to listen twice to find the chords and melody.

The box of the instrument is entirely of wood, with a cunning of construction having had centuries of study, rehearsal, and try-out by Italians, Spaniards, and the same Arabians who hunted up the Arabic numerals.

At music stores and pawn shops the instrument is called a guitar, a GUITAR.

The banjo is meant for jigs, buck and wing dances,

attack, surprise, riot and rout. The guitar is intended for serenades, croons, for retreat, retirement, fadeaways.

I thank you.

Carl Sandburg

# P. G. Wodehouse

IN 1931, P. G. WODEHOUSE was a guest of the estimable Citizen Hearst. Stories about the bizarre behavior of the multimillionaire abounded throughout his career, and Wodehouse added to the heap. He wrote to his friend William Townend:

February 25, 1931

Dear Bill:

Since I last wrote, I have been spending a week at Hearst's ranch. He owns 400,000 acres, more than the whole of Long Island. . . .

Meals take place in an enormous room hung with banners, and are served at a long table, with Hearst sitting in the middle on one side and Marion Davies in the middle on the other. The longer you're there, the further you get from the middle. I sat on Marion's right the first night, then found myself getting edged further and further away, till I got to the extreme end, when I thought it time to leave. Another day and I should have been feeding on the floor.

# F. Scott Fitzgerald

WHEN HE WAS a mere twenty-three, F. Scott Fitzgerald wrote the following unorthodox letter of inquiry to an editor at Charles Scribner's Sons. It was 1919, the heyday of *Scribner's Magazine*, a literary review.

Dear Mr. Bridges:

This is a query. I have a project. It is a work of about 20,000 words and more on the order of a novel than like these stories I've been doing. But it's the sort of thing that will require a full month's work and as *The New Republic, Scribner's*, and possibly the *Atlantic Monthly* are the only magazines that would publish it I don't want to start until you assure me that there's *nothing* in the project which seems to bar it from *Scribner's* if it be *sufficiently* interesting and well done.

It is a literary forgery purporting to be selections from the notebook of a man who is a complete literary radical. . . .

It will be in turns cynical, ingenuous, life-saturated, critical, and bitter. It will be racy and startling with opinions and personalities. . . .

Of course you can't possibly commit yourself until you've seen it but as I say I'd want to know before I start if a work of that nature would be intrinsically hostile to the policy of *Scribner's Magazine.* . . .

⌒

Fitzgerald and his good friend, writer Andrew Turnbull, tried to outdo each other in a long stream of correspondence by using increasingly obscure Shakespearean words. Abruptly, Fitzgerald turned the tables and wrote "Andronio" the following letter, proffering advice in the crassest American slang he could muster:

August 18, 1932
Dear Andronio:

Upon mature consideration I advise you to go no farther with your vocabulary. If you have a lot of words they will become like some muscles you have developed that you are compelled to use, and you must use this one in expressing yourself or in criticizing others. It is hard to say who will punish you the most for this, the dumb people who don't know what you are talking about or the learned ones who do. But wallop you they will and you will be forced to confine yourself to pen and paper.

Then you will be a writer and may God have mercy on your soul.

No! A thousand times no! Far, far better confine yourself to a few simple expressions in life, the ones that served billions upon countless billions of our forefathers and still serve admirably all but a tiny handful of those at present clinging to the earth's crust. Here are the only expressions you need:

*"Yeah"*
*"Naw"*
*"Gimme de meat"*

and you need at least one good *bark* (we all need one good bark) such as:

*"I'll knock your back teeth down your throat!"*

So forget all that has hitherto attracted you in our complicated system of grunts and go back to those fundamental ones that have stood the test of time.

With warm regards to you all,
Scott F.

⌒

Fitzgerald once—more than once—exploded in a rage at a party. In this case, it was a tea party given by a Mrs. Bayard Turnbull in May 1934. We can only guess what a Mrs. Perce said at the gathering that so enraged Fitzgerald, but here is his letter of apology to his hostess:

Dear Margaret:

I know it was very annoying for me to have lost my temper in public and I want to apologize to you both, for the discomfort that I know I gave you. There are certain subjects that *simply do not belong to an afternoon tea* and, while I still think that Mrs. Perce's arguments were almost maddening enough to justify homicide, I appreciate that it was no role of mine to intrude my intensity of feeling upon a group who had expected a quiet tea party.

Ever yours faithfully,

Scott Fitzgerald

During his Hollywood years, Fitzgerald wrote the following peculiar letter to his landlady:

1403 North Laurel Avenue

Hollywood, California

July 29, 1940

Dear Mrs. Neuville:

I thought the other day that a large rat had managed to insert itself into the plaster above my bedroom and workroom. I was, however, surprised that it apparently slept at night and worked in the day, causing its greatest din around high noon.

However yesterday, much to my surprise, I deduced from the sounds it emitted that it was a dog, or rather several dogs, and evidently training for a race, for they ran round and round the tin roof. Now I don't know how these greyhounds climbed up the wall but I know dog racing is against the law of

California—so I thought you'd like to know. Beneath the arena where these races occur an old and harassed literary man is gradually going mad.

Sincerely,

F. Scott Fitzgerald

# Ernest Hemingway

FROM THEIR MID-TWENTIES, F. Scott Fitzgerald and Ernest Hemingway were good friends, despite the intense contrast in their worldviews and general preferences. By the time both were thirty, they were world-famous for their writing.

In 1925, Hemingway wrote Fitzgerald a jocose letter discussing, in part, their differences:

Burguete, Spain
Dear Scott:

. . . I am feeling better than I've ever felt—haven't drunk anything but wine since I left Paris. God it has been wonderful country. But you hate country. All right omit description of country. I wonder what your idea of heaven would be—A beautiful vacuum filled with wealthy monogamists, all powerful and members of the best families all drinking themselves to death. And hell would probably [be] an ugly vacuum full of poor polygamists unable to obtain booze or with chronic stomach disorders that they called secret sorrows.

To me heaven would be a big bull ring with me holding two barrera seats and a trout stream outside that no one else was allowed to fish in and two lovely houses in the town; one where I would have my wife and children and be monogamous and love them truly and well and the other where I would have my nine

beautiful mistresses on 9 different floors and one house
would be fitted up with special copies of the *Dial*
printed on soft tissue and kept in the toilets on every
floor and in the other house we would use the *American
Mercury* and the *New Republic*. Then there would be a
fine church like in Pamplona where I could go and be
confessed on the away from one house to the other and
I would get on my horse and ride out with my son to
my bull ranch named Hacienda Hadley and toss coins
to all my illegitimate children that lived [on] the road. I
would write out at the Hacienda and send my son in to
lock the chastity belts onto my mistresses because
someone had just galloped up with the news that a
notorious monogamist named Fitzgerald had been seen
riding toward the town at the head of a company of
strolling drinkers. . . .

Yours,

Ernest

Hemingway's career as a writer was riddled with dry spells.
Here's how he turned down his friend Thomas Shevlin's invitation to participate in a fishing tournament after the
muse came through for him:

Dear Tommy:

It's so hard to write this that I've been trying to do
it for five days and haven't been able to.

Listen, kid, I can't come and fish on your team in

the tournament. I know that is ratting out and I tell you as soon as possible so that you will be able to get another fisherman.

This is how it is. I went to Cuba intending to write three stories. I wrote the first one and it was good. Then I started on the second one and before I knew it I had fifteen thousand words done and was going better than I have gone since *Farewell To Arms* and I knew it was a novel.

So there it is. I can't be a sportsman and write a novel at the same time. I've had such stinko luck on fish that it's probably an asset for you not to have me. But I would have loved to fish with you and with Hugo.

Yours always,

Papa

# Writers in Hollywood

THE FAMOUS INCURSION of writers in Hollywood began as soon as sound films caught on. A trail of funny letters also began.

Here's a telegram from the early 1920s that writer Herman Mankiewicz (who went on to cowrite *Citizen Kane*) sent to his friend and fellow writer Ben Hecht:

> Will you accept $300 per week to work for Paramount Pictures? All expenses paid. The $300 is peanuts. Millions are to be grabbed out here and your only competition is idiots. Don't let this get around.

Nine years later, Hollywood's attitude toward writers hadn't changed. (Some maintain that it remains the same today.) Raymond Chandler wrote the following to Charles Morton, the associate editor of *Atlantic Monthly*, a month after the magazine had published his exposé of Hollywood and its misuses of writers:

> Dear Charles:
>
> I've owed you a letter for so damn long that I suppose you wonder whether I'm still alive. So do I, at times. Before I delve into your two letters to see if there are any questions you wanted replies to, let me

report that my blast at Hollywood was received here in frozen silence. . . . My agent was told by the Paramount story editor that it had done me a lot of harm with the producers at Paramount. Charles Brackett, that fading wit, said: "Chandler's books are not good enough, nor his pictures bad enough, to justify that article." I wasted a little time trying to figure out what that meant. It seems to mean that the only guy who can speak his mind about Hollywood is either (a) a failure in Hollywood, or (b) a celebrity somewhere else. I would reply to Mr. Brackett that if my books had been any worse, I should not have been invited to Hollywood, and that if they had been any better, I should not have come.

# Eugene O'Neill

"LIGHTHEARTED" is approximately the last word that could be used to describe playwright Eugene O'Neill. Yet that's the tone of this letter he wrote to a Professor William Lyon Phelps, who had invited him to deliver a lecture:

October 27, 1922
My dear Professor Phelps:

I am very grateful to you for the honor of your invitation but I have never lectured and don't believe I ever will. Frankly, there is a certain prejudice in my mind against it. It seems to me that authors should neither be seen nor heard outside of their work—(not this one, at any rate, for I'm quite certain my plays act better than I ever could—which is faint praise for them indeed!). So, both from the standpoint of personal discretion and of Christian charity toward the audience, I feel bound to decline.

But again, all gratitude to you for the honor of selecting me. I appreciate that immensely and regret that I cannot accept.

# Alexander Woollcott

CRITIC AND SATIRIST Alexander Woollcott was a most amusing, if often perplexing, fellow. One isn't sure between which lines to read in this letter to Margaret Mitchell:

Bomoseen, Vt.
August 7, 1936
My dear Miss Mitchell:

I have just finished reading *Gone With the Wind* and found it completely absorbing. Its narrative has the directness and gusto of Dumas. I enjoyed it enormously. I was almost through it when I said to myself: "God's nightgown! This must be the Peg Mitchell who wrote me once about the little girl who swallowed a water moccasin and the tall man in the wrinkled nurse's uniform who thronged the road from Atlanta to Miami." Is it?

If your royalties have begun to come in, kindly send a large share of them as per the enclosed instructions and oblige

A. Woollcott

Apparently, no venue was too small to escape Woollcott's attention. And wrath. Here's a letter he wrote to the Omaha *World Herald*:

San Mateo, Calif.

December 19, 1935

Dear Sir,

May I not, as the late Woodrow Wilson used to say, call your attention to an editorial which appeared in your issue of December 9th under the caption "The Woollcott Menace"? It has found its way out to me here in San Mateo, out in the great open spaces where men are menace. And as it reiterates a frequently repeated allegation, I am experimenting, for the first time in some years, in the luxury of answering it—for publication or not, as you see fit.

It is the substance of this editorial that as a recommender of books over the radio, I take advantage of a nationwide network to further the sale of soft, sentimental works. "Marshmallows" was the term employed. Since this series of broadcasts began, I have cast my oral vote for the following works:

*Paths of Glory*, by Humphrey Cobb
*Life with Father*, by Clarence Day
*North to the Orient*, by Anne Morrow Lindbergh
*Valiant Is the Word for Carrie*, by Barry Benefield
*I Write as I Please*, by Walter Duranty
*The Woollcott Reader*, an anthology of seventeen
    authors ranging from J. M. Barrie to Evelyn
    Waugh.

In addition to these there have been brief parenthetical bursts of applause for

*Death and General Putnam*, by Arthur Guiterman
*Mrs. Astor's Horse*, by Stanley Walker

It is quite impossible for any literate adult to think that this list represents pink publications for pale people. If these be "marshmallows," then I am the Grand Duchess Marie.

What interests me in this instance is the apparent lack of journalistic conscience manifested by the editorial I complain of. If that editorial was written by someone who would think of that list as so many marshmallows, it was the work of a fool. If it was written by someone who was not even familiar with what books I had recommended, it was the work of a knave. Neither alternative is agreeable for a colleague to contemplate. Of course, there is always the third possibility that your editorial writer is a nicely balanced mixture of the two.

Yours sincerely,
Alexander Woollcott

Woollcott wrote to his friend Marian Stoll in 1942, prankishly from:

The White House

January 21, 1942

Dear Marian:

Under separate cover (which has always been our life in a nutshell) I have sent you two packs of playing cards because:

(a) you said you wanted some
(b) these, which were given me for Xmas, are not the kind I like and
(c) they can be washed with soap and water.

Personally I prefer washing my hands instead of the cards. I never soil cards because my hands are always pure, like my thoughts.

Your old playmate,

Alexander Woollcott

# Dorothy Parker

DOROTHY PARKER sent the following telegram to a friend who had just had a baby after enduring a long, widely publicized pregnancy:

Good work, Mary. We all knew you had it in you.

# Carl Sandburg

IN A LETTER to his friend and fellow punster, Kenneth Holden, Carl Sandburg told this anecdote:

May 19, 1945
Dear Ken:

Did you hear about the Nazi in Magdeburg who crept into a bomb-washed store where once in the heil-hitler days they sold picture frames and the poor goddamn Nazi licked off a mouthful of gold leaf from one of the frames? Two MPs watched him shiver in his guts and crumple up and die and one of the MPs said, "Suicide" and the other MP, "How could a little gold leaf like that kill a guy?" and the first one, "It wasn't so much the gold leaf as he was smitten with a sense of inner gilt."

And you may be sure I hope and trust that we go on being a couple of sons of puns.

As Ever,
Carl

# Robert Benchley

WHEN THE CELEBRATED HUMORIST Robert Benchley visited Venice, Italy, for the first time, he immediately dispatched a telegram to a friend. It has since become a classic:

STREETS FULL OF WATER. PLEASE ADVISE.
ROBERT BENCHLEY

# James Thurber and Samuel Goldwyn

JAMES THURBER'S short story "The Secret Life of Walter Mitty" became so well known that Hollywood producer Samuel Goldwyn decided that he wanted Thurber to be a writer on his staff. But Thurber was perfectly happy where he was, writing for *The New Yorker* and its famous editor Harold Ross. Thurber had absolutely no interest in going into the movie business. Goldwyn wrote him:

I'll pay you $500 a week.

Thurber replied:

Sorry, but Mr. Ross has met the increase.

A series of exchanges ensued. Each time Goldwyn wrote, he offered Thurber more money, first $1,000 a week, then $1,500, and finally $2,500. Each time he got the same reply from Thurber:

Mr. Ross has met the increase.

After a long delay, Goldwyn wrote again, but this time, for some unknown reason, the offer had dropped back to $1,500. Thurber's reply:

I'm sorry, but Mr. Ross has met the decrease.

# James Thurber

Two New Orleans belles wrote to editor Ross in 1949 asking for a photograph of Thurber. Ross dutifully forwarded the letter to the author in Connecticut. Thurber replied:

Dear ladies:

Harold Ross, a timid man who is easily terrified, sent your letter on to me and I have been picking it up and putting it down. Nobody has been interested in my looks for a long time, including myself. I don't have any pictures around, and I haven't had any taken for many years, except by newspaper photographers and the like. Maybe a couple will turn up one of these days, and so I will keep your letter on file in a folder all by itself. Ross has a far more interesting face and there ought to be photographs of him in your city, since he worked on a newspaper there years ago. I am delighted, of course, that two southern belles know their way around in my books and would like to know what kind of man acts that way. Everybody else is writing for pictures of Montgomery Clift.

Best wishes to you both.
Sincerely yours,
James Thurber

A pair of avid Thurber readers wrote to ask him why he wrote what he wrote. His reply:

You can tell where I get my ideas from the things I write, and then you will know as much about it as I do. To write about people you have to know people, to write about bloodhounds you have to know bloodhounds, to write about the Loch Ness monster you have to find out about it. I write because I have to write and it's a good thing a writer gets paid. If I juggled because I have to juggle I couldn't live. You will have to ask my readers why they read what I write. I hope they read it because it has something to say. You can also say that writers could get more written if they didn't have to answer so many questions about why they write.

Best wishes.

Sincerely yours,

James Thurber

Here is Thurber's humorous, avuncular letter to a Manhattan schoolchild named Robert Leifert, who wrote to request assistance on a school project.

Dear Robert:

Since a hundred schoolchildren a year write me letters like yours—some writers get a thousand— the problem of what to do about such classroom "projects" has become a serious one for all of us. If a writer answered all of you he would get nothing else done. When I was a baby goat I had to do all my own research on projects, and I enjoyed doing it. I never wrote an author for his autograph or photograph in my life. Photographs are for movie actors to send to girls. Tell your teacher I said so, and please send me her name. . . .

One of the things that discourage us writers is the fact that 90 percent of you children write wholly, or partly, illiterate letters, carelessly typed. You yourself write "clarr" for "class" and that's a honey, Robert, since "s" is next to "a," and "r" is the line above. Most schoolchildren in America would do a dedication like the following (please find the mistakes in it and write me about them):

> *To Miss Effa G. Burns*
> *without who's help*
> *this book could never*
> *of been finished it,*
> *is dedicated with*
> *gartitude by it's*
> *arthur.*

Show that to your teacher and tell her to show it to her principal and see if they can find the mistakes. . . .

Just yesterday a letter came in from a girl your age in South Carolina asking for biographical material and photograph. That is not the kind of education they have in Russia, we are told, because it's too much like a hobby or waste of time. What do you and your classmates want to be when you grow up—collectors? Then who is going to keep the United States ahead of Russia in science, engineering, and the arts?

Please answer this letter. If you don't I'll write to another pupil.

Sincerely yours,

James Thurber

A representative of the Harvard Business School wrote Thurber in 1961 (the year he died) asking him to give a guest lecture. By that time Thurber, in his late sixties, was almost completely blind. He replied, from London:

I had to give up public appearances when I became a hundred and went blind nearly twenty years ago, and, besides, I am now in Europe and in the Fall expect to be in Jeopardy.

Thanks anyway, and all best wishes. . . .

# William Faulkner

WILLIAM FAULKNER had a complicated, difficult life, which began with a thorny childhood and adolescence. He dropped in and out of schools, then the RAF (the U.S. Army wouldn't have him), served as a postmaster and a scoutmaster, writing all the while. For the last half of 1925, when he was twenty-eight, Faulkner took the Grand Tour of Western Europe. He wrote his mother the following:

> Dear Moms,
>
> England was too dear for me. I walked some, saw quite a bit of the loveliest, quietest country under the sun, and have spent the last two days on a Breton fishing boat—a tub of a thing that rocks and rolls in a dead calm. We made a good haul, though, including two three-foot sharks which they killed with boat hooks. These people eat anything though: I don't doubt but what I've eaten shark without knowing it, and liked it. A French cook can take an old shoe and make it taste good.

Faulkner was noted for his reclusive, withdrawn nature. He lived in Oxford, Mississippi, and among his few close friends was the critic and writer Malcolm Cowley. He and

Faulkner corresponded for many years, and in this letter Faulkner showed a rare sardonic sense of humor.

Oxford, Miss.
16 July [1948]
Dear Brother Cowley:

I had a letter from a Mr. Pearson at New Haven about coming there to make a talk, something. I have lost it and cant answer. He spoke of you in the letter; will you either send me his address or if you correspond with him my apologies for losing the address and that I don't think I know anything worth 200 dollars worth talking about but I hope to be up East this fall though I still don't believe I will know anything to talk about worth 200 dollars so I would probably settle for a bottle of good whiskey.

If I come up, I would like to see you.
Faulkner

Faulkner once served as postmaster at the University of Mississippi. He decided to quit his job and tersely explained his reason for doing so in the following letter to the Postmaster General in Washington:

As long as I live under the capitalist system, I expect to have my life influenced by the demands of moneyed people. But I will be damned if I propose to be at the beck and call of every itinerant scoundrel who has two cents to invest in a postage stamp. This, sir, is my resignation.

William Faulkner

A Dr. Julius S. Bixler of Colby College invited Faulkner to receive an honorary degree in 1956. Faulkner's response:

Dear Dr. Bixler:

Your letter of February 20th was at hand when I reached home today.

I thank the Board of Trustees of Colby College very much for the honor proffered me, which I must decline for the following reason. I did not attend school long enough to receive even a certificate of graduation from elementary school. For me to receive an honorary degree from Colby College would be an insult to all those who have gained degrees by means of the long and arduous devotion commensurate with what any degree must be always worth.

Thank you again for the honor proffered me.

# E. B. White

ESSAYIST, NOVELIST, and grammarian E. B. White wrote this consummate letter of indignation to Con Ed, in response to a letter that would certainly alarm anyone:

December 21, 1951
Dear Mr. Aiken:

I am a stockholder in the Consolidated Edison Company, and I rent an apartment at 229 East 48 Street in which there is a gas refrigerator. So I have a double interest in your letter of December 19. It seems to me a very odd letter indeed.

You say that my refrigerator, even if it seems to be operating properly, may be producing poison gas, and you suggest that I open a window. I do not want to open a window. It would be a very unpopular move with the cook. Furthermore, I haven't the slightest intention of living under the same roof with a machine that discharges poison gas. Your recommendation is that I get plenty of fresh air— enough to counteract the effect of the gas. But I cannot believe that you are serious.

Will you be good enough to let me know what sort of poison gas is generated by a Servel gas refrigerator, and in what quantity, and how discharged. I know that there is a vent at the top of the machine and that some sort of warm air flows from the vent. I have always assumed it was hot air. Is it something else?

I also know that a gas refrigerator poses a carbon problem, and I ask the landlord to remove the carbon about once a year, which he does. But your letter makes me think that the matter is not so simple and I am anxious to be enlightened.

If gas refrigerators are, as your letter suggests, discharging poison gases into people's homes I don't want to own a gas refrigerator and I shall certainly sell my stock.

Here's White's succinct, if cryptic, reply to an invitation extended by a Mr. J. Donald Adams:

September 28, 1956
Dear Mr. Adams:
Thanks for your letter inviting me to join the committee of the Arts and Sciences for Eisenhower.
I must decline, for secret reasons.
Sincerely,
E. B. White

White was once accused by the ASPCA of dodging tax on his dog. Here is his rankled and witty reply:

12 April 1951

Dear Sirs:

I have your letter, undated, saying that I am harboring an unlicensed dog in violation of the law. If by "harboring" you mean getting up two or three times every night to pull Minnie's blanket up over her, I am harboring a dog all right. The blanket keeps slipping off. I suppose you are wondering by now why I don't get her a sweater instead. That's a joke on you. She has a knitted sweater, but she doesn't like to wear it for sleeping; her legs are so short they work out of a sweater and her toenails get caught in the mesh, and this disturbs her rest. If Minnie doesn't get her rest, she feels it right away. I do myself, and of course with this night duty of mine . . . I haven't had any real rest in years. Minnie is twelve.

In spite of what your inspector reported, she has a license. She is licensed in the state of Maine as an unspayed bitch, or what is more commonly called an "unspaded" bitch. She wears her metal license tag but I must say I don't particularly care for it, as it is in the shape of a hydrant, which seems to me a feeble gag, besides being pointless in the case of a female. It is hard to believe that any state in the Union would circulate a gag like that and make people pay money for it, but Maine is always thinking of something. Maine puts up roadside crosses along the highway to mark the spots where people have lost their lives in motor accidents, so the highways are beginning to take on the appearance of a cemetery, and motoring in Maine has become a solemn experience, when one thinks mostly about death. I was driving along a road near Kittery the other day thinking about death and all of a sudden I heard the spring peepers. That changed me right away and I suddenly thought about life. It was the nicest feeling.

You asked about Minnie's name, sex, breed, and phone number. She doesn't answer the phone. She is a dachshund and can't reach it, but she wouldn't answer it even if she could, as she has no interest in outside calls. I did have a dachshund once, a male, who was interested in the telephone, and who got a great many calls, but Fred was an exceptional dog (his name was Fred) and I can't think of anything offhand that he wasn't interested in. The telephone was only one of a thousand things. He loved life— that is, he loved life if by "life" you mean "trouble," and of course the phone is almost synonymous with trouble. Minnie loves life, too, but her idea of life is a warm bed, preferably with an electric pad, and a friend in bed with her, and plenty of shut-eye, night and day. She's almost twelve. I guess I've already mentioned that. I got her from Dr. Clarence Little in 1939. He was using dachshunds in his cancer-research experiments (that was before Winchell was running the thing) and he had a couple of extra puppies, so I wheedled Minnie out of him. She later had puppies by her own father, at Dr. Little's request. What do you think about that for a scandal? I know what Fred thought about it. He was some put out.

Sincerely yours,

E. B. White

# John Cheever

SPEAKING OF ANIMALS, in 1961 John Cheever and his wife, Mary, were asked by their friend, writer Josephine Herbst, to take care of her cat. Cheever and the cat hated each other. The cat was a male whom Cheever named Delmore for the lugubrious poet Delmore Schwartz, and when the day came that Delmore began spraying the walls, Cheever promptly took him to the vet to be neutered.

After two years with Delmore, Cheever decided it was time to write Herbst an update:

Dear Josie:

It's been years since we had anything but the most sketchy communication. . . . I've long since owed you an account of the destiny of your cat and here we go.

The cat, after your leaving him, seemed not certain of his character or his place and we changed his name to Delmore which immediately made him more vivid. The first sign of his vividness came when he dumped a load in a Kleenex box while I was suffering from a cold. During a paroxysm of sneezing I grabbed for some Kleenex. I shall not overlook my own failures in this tale but when I got the cat shit off my face and the ceiling I took Delmore to the kitchen door and drop-kicked him into the clothesyard. This was an intolerable cruelty and I have not yet been forgiven. He is not a forgiving cat. Indeed he is proud. Spring came on then and as I was about to remove [one of] the clear glass storm window[s], Delmore, thinking the window to be open, hurled himself against the glass. This hurt his nose and his psyche badly. Mary and the children then went to the Mountains and I spent a reasonably happy summer cooking for Delmore. The next eventfulness came on Thanksgiving. When the family had gathered for dinner and I was about to carve the turkey there came a strangling noise from the bathroom. I ran there and found Delmore sitting in the toilet, neck-deep in cold water and very sore. I got him out and dried him with towels but there was no forgiveness. Shortly after Christmas a Hollywood writer and his wife came to lunch. My usual salutation to Delmore is: Up yours, and when the lady heard me say this she scorned me and gathered Delmore to her breasts. Delmore, in a flash, started to unscrew her right eyeball and the lady, trying to separate herself from Delmore lost a big piece of an Italian dress she was wearing which Mary said cost $250.00. This was not held against Delmore and a few days later when we had a skating party I urged Delmore to come to the pond with us. He seemed pleased and frisked along like a family-loving cat but at that moment a little wind came from the northeast and spilled the snow off a hemlock onto Delmore. He gave me a dirty look, went back to the house and dumped another load in the Kleenex box. This time he got the cleaning woman and they remain unfriendly.

This is not meant at all to be a rancorous account and I think Delmore enjoys himself. . . . People who dislike me go directly to his side and he is, thus, a peace-maker. He loves to play with toilet paper. He does not like catnip mice. He does not kill song birds. In the spring the rabbits chase him around the lawn but they leave after the lettuce has been eaten and he has the terrace pretty much to himself. He is very fat these days and his step, Carl Sandburg notwithstanding, sounds more like that of a barefoot middle-aged man on his way to the toilet than the settling in of a winter fog but he has his role and we all respect it and here endeth my report on Delmore the cat.

Best,

John

# Flannery O'Connor

FLANNERY O'CONNOR, the great Southern author of novels, novellas, and short fiction, wrote this letter to her friend Cecil Dawkins:

Dear Cecil:

Well my novel is finished.

The current ordeal is that my mother is now in the process of reading it. She reads about two pages, gets up and goes to the back door for a conference with Shot [their dog], comes back, reads two more pages, gets up and goes to the barn. Yesterday she read a whole chapter. There are twelve chapters. All the time she is reading, I know she would like to be in the yard digging. I think the reason I am a short-story writer is so my mother can read my work in one sitting.

In 1961, O'Connor wrote her friend "A" about the confusion that her book titles are capable of causing, particularly her 1960 novel *The Violent Bear It Away*.

Some friends of mine in Texas wrote me that a friend of theirs went into a bookstore looking for a paperback copy of *A Good Man* [*Is Hard to Find*]. The clerk said, "We don't have that one but we have another by that author, called *The Bear That Ran Away With it*. I foresee the trouble I am going to have with *Everything That Rises Must Converge—Every Rabbit That Rises Is a Sage*.

## *Isaac Asimov*

<small>SCIENCE FICTION AUTHOR</small> Isaac Asimov wrote an admiring letter to science writer Carl Sagan in December 1974:

> Dear Carl,
>
> I have just finished *The Cosmic Connection* and loved every word of it. You are my idea of a good writer because you have an unmannered style, and when I read what you write, I hear you talking.
>
> One more thing about the book made me nervous. It was entirely too obvious that you are smarter than I am. I hate that.

# S. J. Perelman

BEST KNOWN TODAY for writing two of the best Marx Brothers movies, *Horse Feathers* and *Monkey Business*, S. J. Perelman was in his day widely renowned as a master of satire and irony. He wrote more than a dozen books, numerous other screenplays, plays, and several volumes of essays. He served as principal arbiter of humor at *The New Yorker* for several decades, and was an icon to generations of humorists.

Perelman's cleverness extended to the simplest of missives, such as this dinner invitation Perelman wrote to essayist, critic, editor, and good friend Edmund Wilson in 1939:

Hotel Fairfax
116 East 56th Street
New York City
February 9, 1939

Dear Edmondo,

I got back from the country to find your card sparkling like a jewel in a diadem of unpaid bills, poison pen letters, and rusty old telephone messages. We would like very much to see you but there is no earthly reason why you should have to bend over a hot stove (with flushed cheeks, occasionally tucking up a wisp of hair on the nape of your neck) to prepare dinner for us. I think it would be much better if Mrs. Wilson and you came in and had dinner with us. This invitation does not extend to your baby, who I understand has a tendency to fall asleep about six o'clock after gorging himself, belching, and generally behaving in the worst possible taste.

Do you have a sitter whom you could call in for the occasion? A father of two since I saw you last, you will find my conversation studded with references to Snuggle-duckies, pablum, and strollers. But why depress you in advance?

We look forward to seeing you just as soon as possible.

Ever,

S. J. Perelman

Perelman was not likely to let anyone get away with anything. Here's a letter he wrote in 1975 to Perry Howze, an aspiring graphic designer and cartoonist who had written a fan letter to Perelman—and misspelled Perelman's name. They later became friends, but not before Perelman penned the following:

Gramercy Park Hotel
New York City

January 1975

Dear Perry,

Judging from your progressive-school handwriting, the content of your previous note, and the imperious tone of the message below, you seem to be a willful infant who is accustomed to getting her own way. Accordingly, you may profit from a word of advice and I'll give it to you for free.

The next time you issue a demand for anything, honey, whether it's a spoonful of farina or a Christmas card, examine the name of the person you're asking and spell it correctly.

Now wipe the egg off your face and have a happy New Year.

Love,

⌒

Perelman had the occasion to write the following letter in 1978 to Arthur H. Rosen, president of the National Committee on United States–China Relations, Inc.:

Gramercy Park Hotel
New York City
July 17, 1978
Dear Sir:

I am in receipt of your boorish little note in which you dub me "an alte knacker" (whatever you conceive that to mean) and a "meshugener" (misspelled though the intent is clear), and equate me with folk seeking to perform rock on the Great Wall and to canoe on the Yangtse. Not content with these gibes at a person unknown to you, you then demand with a cackle whether I consider myself a comedian. All the foregoing, please note, on the basis of a telephone inquiry reported to you by a subordinate, the details of which you know nothing about.

Let me, therefore, reply as succinctly as I can. I have never before heard of you, but if the above is indicative of your skill at furthering relations between the United States and China, you are lamentably miscast. You belong on the borscht circuit—not at Grossinger's, the Concord Hotel, or even at Kutscher's, but at some lesser establishment where the clientele is as gross and chuckle-headed as you are. It defies reason that the promotion of cordiality between two great nations should have been entrusted to an asshole.

Yours, etc.

# Quentin Crisp

THE ESTEEMED AUTHOR, actor, raconteur, and noted wit Quentin Crisp, who described himself on his calling card as a "retired waif," didn't make it to New York for the first time until he was in his seventies, but, as he often said ever afterward, "The moment I saw New York, I wanted it." He was able to move there to do his one-man show, *An Evening with Quentin Crisp*, and he enjoyed considerable celebrity for the rest of his many days.

Shortly after he first arrived in New York, he wrote the following letter to his young niece Denise:

The Church of the Beloved Disciple,
348 West 14th. St
New York City
23rd. October '80

Thank you, Dear Denise, for your kind letter. I am not really staying in a church but it is a safer resting place for letters than my rather dubious room opposite. I have, as you see, reached America and am hammering away at a Mrs. Levitt who is my immigration lawyer in the hope of becoming a "resident alien." At the moment our plea is that I will do work that no American will do. If this fails, I shall "come here to join my relatives." Mrs G. now has a telephone and we have spoken to each other at great length. She is planning to visit New York in order to witness me when I do a stint of addressing the multitude in a dim bar on 6th. Avenue. How she will return in the middle of the night to New Jersey I have no idea but, as you know, she is infinitely resourceful and will doubtless have a distant relative in New York whom she can nag into allowing her to sleep on his bathroom floor.

At the moment I am staying in a penthouse that belongs to a kind friend. The hospitality of Americans is infinite. Taxi drivers are willing to take you round the city free of charge; bus drivers shake you by the hand; pedestrians say, "Welcome to the United States!"

If you possibly can, you should come here though I am aware of your difficulties. Everyone is rich and everyone is handsome so you could marry almost anybody within a week.

I was delighted to hear from you and sorry that most of your correspondence is with my agent. I send you my best wishes for your health and happiness. This message also goes for your mother and your children. If I am granted residency here, I will write again; if not, the whole world will know. . . .

Quentin

P.S. Take no notice of the back of this page; it is only part of a rejected book.

Q.C.

## Andy Rooney

ANDY ROONEY, whom we'll return to in the next section, once got a rave review for one of his books in the *Washington Journalism Review*. He immediately wrote the reviewer:

> Roger Piantadosi
> *Washington Journalism Review*
> Dear Roger,
>    Bad taste though it may be, I can't resist telling you that I could hardly have been more pleased with your review of my book than if I'd written the review myself.
>    I admire writers who don't care what people say about their work but I am not among them. I care desperately. I consider myself a minor writer for this reason. J. D. Salinger is a major writer. He doesn't care. Of course, he doesn't write anything either.

An editor at Warner Books wrote what Rooney thought was a good letter, asking him to contribute to a book they were going to publish called *The Joy of Pigging Out*. Rooney wrote back:

Patti Breitman
Editor
Warner Books
Dear Patti,

Thanks for your understanding letter. What you seemed to understand was that I probably wouldn't do what you were asking me to. That was good thinking on your part.

There is just so much Andy Rooney the world needs and having my name on the cover of a book and included in the publicity when I've had almost nothing to do with it, is the kind of step toward exceeding that need that I try not to take.

*The Joy of Pigging Out* sounds like fun but I hope the phrase "pigging out" isn't past its prime. It reached its peak with teenagers about ten years ago and, if you're lucky, they may all be of book-buying age now and it won't occur to them, at least, that the phrase has been phased out of the lexicon of the current crop.

Good luck but don't wait for a contribution from me.

Sincerely,
Andy Rooney

# III

# DENIZENS OF THE FINE ARTS
# AND SHOW BUSINESS

*There's no business like show business, unless it is the arts.*
*You cannot tell where one begins and the other starts.*
*If you would like to know an artist or performer better,*
*Forget the art, forget the show, and go right to a letter.*
*A letter being personal is always less inhibited*
*Than the show that is put on or art that is exhibited.*
*Creative people have great gifts which some regard as flaws;*
*What they crave most in this life is approval and applause.*

CHARLES OSGOOD

# Mozart

WHEN HE WAS twenty-one, Wolfgang Amadeus Mozart wrote this letter to his father after spending an evening visiting a friend whose daughter was reputedly a child prodigy. Although the little girl's piano technique had been admired and resoundingly praised by many musicians, Mozart (who, of course, had himself been one of the greatest child prodigies in history) regarded her talent somewhat differently.

Augsburg
October 23, 1777
*Mon très cher Père:*

. . . When I was at Stein's house the other day he put before me a sonata by Beecke—I think I have told you that already. That reminds me, now for his little daughter. Anyone who sees and hears her play and can keep from laughing must, like her father, be made of stone. For instead of sitting in the middle of the clavier, she sits right opposite the treble, as it gives her more chance of flopping about and making grimaces. If it has to be played a third time, then she plays it even more slowly. When a passage is being played the arm must be raised as high as possible, and according as the notes in the passage are stressed, the arm, not the fingers, must do this, and that too with great emphasis in a heavy and clumsy manner. But the best joke of all is that when she comes to a passage which ought to flow like oil and which necessitates a change of finger, she does not bother her head about it, but when the moment arrives, she just leaves out the notes, raises her hand, and starts off again quite comfortably—a method by which she is much more likely to strike a wrong note, which often produces a curious effect.

. . . Herr Stein is quite crazy about his daughter, who is eight-and-a-half and who now learns everything by heart. She may succeed, for she has a great talent for music. But she will not make progress by this method—for she will never acquire great rapidity, since she definitely does all she can to make her hands heavy. Further, she will never acquire the most essential, the most difficult and the chief requisite of music, which is *time*, because from her earliest year she has done her utmost *not* to play in time. . . .

Wolfgang Amadeus Mozart

The following year (1778), Mozart wrote to an apparently unduly neglected cousin:

Mademoiselle, my very dear Cousin,
You may perhaps believe, or opine, that I am

dead!—that I am defunct!—or insane!—but no, I beg you to think no such thing, for to think is one thing and to do another! How could I write so beautifully if I were dead? Tell me now, would it be possible? I will not offer a word of apology for my long silence, for you would never believe me; though what is true *is* true! I have had so much to do that I have had time to *think* of my little cousin but not to *write* to her, consequently I have had to leave it undone. Now, however, I do myself the honor of inquiring how you are and how you do? . . .

*Adieu* little coz. I am, I was, I should be, I have been, I had been, I should have been, oh, if I only were, oh, that I were, would God I were; I could be, I shall be, if I were to be, oh, that I might be, I would have been, oh, had I been, oh, that I had been, would God I had been—what? A dried cod! *Adieu ma chère Cousine*, whither away? I am your faithful cousin,

Wolfgang Amadeus Mozart

## *Beethoven*

LUDWIG VAN BEETHOVEN had very little—if any—control over his temper, which swung wildly in all directions. Here are two brief missives that Beethoven wrote on consecutive days to pianist/composer Johann Nepomuk Hummel in 1799. First:

> Never come near me again! You are a faithless cur, and may the hangman take all faithless curs.
> Beethoven

The very next day:

> My dearest Nazerl,
> You are an honest fellow and I now perceive you were right; so come to see me this afternoon; Schuppanzigh will be here too, and the pair of us will scold you, cuff you, and shake you to your heart's content.
> A warm embrace from
> Your Beethoven
> Also known as Little Dumpling

Here's a humorously peevish missive Beethoven wrote to a potential patron, Franz Anton Hoffmeister, regarding a commission that obviously severely displeased the composer, whose unruly feelings about Napoleon Bonaparte moved him to dedicate his *Third Symphony* to him, and later tear off the title page in a rage and retitle the symphony *Eroica*, and rededicate it to the memory of a hero.

April 8, 1802

May the devil ride the whole lot of you, gentlemen—what, suggest to me that I should write a sonata of that sort? At the time of the revolutionary fever—well, at that time it would have been worth considering, but now that everything is trying to get back into the old rut, Bonaparte has made his concordat with the Pope—a sonata of that sort? If at least it were a *Missa pro Sancta Marai a tre voci* or a Vespers, etc.—well, in that case I should immediately take hold of the brush and write down a *Credo in unum* in enormous notes weighing a pound each—but good heavens, a sonata of that sort at the beginning of the new Christian age—ho ho!—count me out of that, for nothing will come of it.

# Chopin

FRÉDÉRIC CHOPIN was hardly the picture of hardiness and good health. But at least he had a sense of humor about it. Here's an excerpt from a letter to his friend Julien Fontana:

December 3, 1838
My Julien:

I have been as sick as a dog for the last fortnight. I had caught cold in spite of the eighteen degrees centigrade, the roses, the orange-trees, the palms, and the fig trees. Three doctors—the most celebrated on the island—examined me. The first said I was going to die, the second that I was actually dying, the third that I was dead already. . . . I had great difficulty in escaping from their bleedings, vesicatories, and packsheets, but thanks be to providence, I am myself again. But my illness was unfavorable to the *Preludes*, which will reach you God knows when. . . .

# George M. Cohan

ACTOR/PRODUCER George M. Cohan was a fabled public speaker. But the day came when he was asked to write a piece for publication in an entertainment magazine. Here's Cohan's reply:

Dear George Buck:

Just received your letter in which you call upon me to write seven or eight hundred words for the anniversary number [of your publication]. Now let me tell you something, kid. Seven or eight hundred are a whole lot of words—I could tell a number of guys what I think of them in less words than that, and also I could do the lyrics of a dozen numbers for a musical play in less words than that. And to be truthful, I don't honestly think I know seven or eight hundred words. There aren't that many words in my entire vocabulary. As a matter of fact, in my whole circle of acquaintances I can't think of any one right now, aside from a few English actors . . . who can spill that many words.

As a dancer, I could never do over three steps. As a composer, I could never find use for over four or five notes in my musical numbers. As a violinist, I could never learn to play above the first position. I'm a one-key piano player, and as a playwright, most of my plays have been presented in two acts for the simple reason that I could seldom think of an idea for a third act. I remember hearing Marcus Loew say one night that he left school as soon as he had learned how to count to ten—he claimed that any learning beyond that was altogether unnecessary. And mind you, that was before he ever became a big moving picture magnate.

I remember an old-time advance agent named Sam Dessauer telling me years ago (he was working for Gus Hill at the time), that Hill hollered so loud about telegrams being sent to him "collect" by his various advance men, that he called them all together one day and insisted that there wasn't anything in the world that couldn't be fully explained in ten words. Of course, they had to sit up nights figuring out how to phrase their messages, but all admitted afterwards that Mr. Hill was absolutely right.

Speaking of words, there are two words necessary to every man's vocabulary—"Yes" and "No." The former is used a great deal out in Hollywood, I understand. When some fellow says, "If you happen to see Mr. So and So, I wish you'd put in a good word for me," does he mean that you should look through Webster's dictionary for a good word or does he mean to actually say something nice about him? If he wants a plug, why doesn't he say so? And when some guy says, "You can take my word for it," why doesn't the guy he says it to ask him what word in the English language is his word? He's made the claim, and he should be challenged. . . .

George M. Cohan

# Groucho Marx

GROUCHO MARX was easily one of the funniest letter writers in history. His wit is as irrepressible and whimsical—and often as denigrating—in his letters as it is in his movies. He was also a wonderful writer and storyteller in general, with a voice as vivid as his characters.

In 1946, when Groucho was an expectant father, he wrote his good friend Irving Hoffman the following letter:

Dear Irving:

Between strokes of good fortune, I have been toying with the idea of making you my impending child's godfather. However, before doing this officially, I would like to see a notarized statement of your overall assets. I don't intend to repeat the unhappy experience that befell my parents late in the 19th century.

At that time there was an Uncle Julius in our family. He was five feet one in his socks, holes and all. He had a brown spade beard, thick glasses, and a head topped off with a bald spot about the size of a buckwheat cake. My mother somehow got the notion that Uncle Julius was wealthy and she told my father, who never did quite understand my mother, that it would be a brilliant piece of strategic flattery were they to make Uncle Julius my godfather.

Well, as happens to all men, I was finally born and

before I could say "Jack Robinson," I was named Julius. At the moment this historic event was taking place, Uncle Julius was in the back room of a cigar store on Third Avenue, dealing them off the bottom. When word reached him that he had been made my godfather, he dropped everything, including two aces he had up his sleeve for an emergency, and quickly rushed over to our flat.

In a speech so moist with emotion that he was blinded by his own eyeglasses, he said that he was overwhelmed by this sentimental gesture on our part and hinted that my future—a rosy one—was irrevocably linked with his. At the conclusion of his speech, still unable to see through his misty lenses, he kissed my father, handed my mother a cigar, and ran back to the pinochle game.

Two weeks later he moved in, paper suitcase and all. As time went by, my mother became suspicious and one day, in discussing him with my father, she not only discovered that Uncle Julius seemed to be without funds, but what was even worse, he owed my father $34.

Since he was only five feet one, my father volunteered to throw him out but my mother advised caution. She said that she had read of many cases where rich men, after living miserly lives, died leaving tremendous fortunes to their heirs.

Uncle Julius remained with us until I got married. By this time, he had the best room in the house and owed my father $84. Shortly after my wedding, my mother finally admitted that Uncle Julius had been a hideous mistake and ordered my father to give him the bum's rush. But Uncle Julius had grown an inch over the years while my father had shrunk proportionately, so he finally convinced my mother that violence was not the solution to the problem.

Soon after this Uncle Julius solved everything by kicking off, leaving me his sole heir. His estate, when probated, consisted of a nine ball that he had stolen from the poolroom, a box of liver pills, and a celluloid dickey.

I suppose I should be more sentimental about the whole thing, but it was a severe shock to all of us, and, if I can help it, it's not going to happen again.

Well Irving, that's the story. If you are interested, let me hear from you as soon as possible and, remember, a financial statement as of today will expedite things considerably.

Regards,
Groucho

---

*Look* magazine staff entertainment writer Leo Rosten wrote a profile of Tallulah Bankhead for the magazine. Groucho took amusing exception with the piece, and he wrote the following letter:

Edwin K. Zittell
Editor
*Look* Magazine
February 1, 1951

Dear Mr. Zittell:

Mr. Leo Rosten writes dazzlingly and engagingly, but unfortunately inaccurately about Miss Bankhead. I know because some weeks ago he wrote about me, and described me as a harum-scarum clown willing and eager to commit any kind of mayhem to get a laugh. Actually I am an elderly student thirsting for learning and solitude, leading an exemplary and sedentary life in a bookish and cloistered atmosphere.

I know Miss Bankhead very well and this full-blown act that she assumes for the press is completely phony. To them she presents herself as a carefree gamin, a social rebel kicking up her heels, frantically dashing from one hot party to another, flouting all the conventions of civilized society just for the hell of it.

This is not the real Tallulah. The one I know is a small-town girl trapped in a profession she loathes, yearning for a touch of the soil; dreaming of a little farm in the backwoods, the gurgle of well water, perhaps a cow or two, a few chickens cackling in the sun, the smell of new-mown hay, and a mate, sunburned and raw-boned, by her side.

In the not too distant future if you happen to drive down Highway Seven between Little Rock and Van Buren and you are hungry for fried possum and corn pone, stop awhile at Bankhead's Beanery. Yes, the motherly little introvert bending over the old wood burner will be the erstwhile madcap Tallulah. And at the cash register you will see the shadow of what was once Groucho Marx. Tell Leo Rosten, your bewildered Boswell, to come down and visit us. He'll get no fried possum and corn pone, but we'll fry the February 13th issue of *Look* and make him eat it word by word.

Sincerely,

Groucho Marx

Groucho's face appeared on the front cover of the December 31, 1951, issue of *Time* magazine. He quickly sent the following hilarious letter to *Time*'s publisher, James A. Linen:

January 4, 1952

Dear Mr. Linen:

The picture of me on the cover of *Time* has changed my entire life. Where formerly my hours were spent playing golf and chasing girls, I now while away the days loitering around Beverly Hills's largest newsstand, selling copies of December 31's issue of *Time* at premium prices.

Admittedly the picture on the cover didn't do me justice (I doubt if any camera could capture my inner beauty), but nevertheless my following is so fanatical that they buy anything that even remotely resembles me. Yesterday, despite the fact that it was raining, I made $13. This is all tax free, for I steal the copies of *Time* while the owner of the newsstand is out eating lunch.

Please use my picture again soon and next time I promise to give you half of everything I get away with.

Cordially,

Groucho Marx

P.S. In addition to Henry James, I also read the *St. Louis Sporting News*.

Groucho's wit was often combined with considerable shrewdness brought about by his vast experience in the entertainment industry.

Here's a priceless letter Groucho wrote to Phil Silvers when Silvers's career finally soared with his appearance in the Broadway smash musical comedy *Top Banana*:

November 15, 1951

Dear Phil:

I won't bore you with the details of how happy I am over your success. You've had it coming. You have been scrambling around near the top for many a year and now at long last you've broken through.

The critics called you a major comic. Well, it couldn't have happened to a nicer guy.

But I must warn you. In a musical, as you know, there are temptations. Thirty or forty beautiful babes in back of you kicking up high—so high that they frequently display sections of their anatomy that in other circles are carefully reserved for the man they ultimately marry. Phil, steer clear of these man-traps. Marry, if you must, but don't marry a chorus girl. As the years roll by you will discover their high kicks grow proportionately lower, and their busts sag just as much as the busts of girls who have never seen the inside of a dressing room.

You may ask then what is the difference? As a veteran of three Broadway musicals, I can quickly tell you chorus girls are notoriously pampered and insolvent. No matter where you take them, they order champagne and chicken à la king. This can be very embarrassing if you are in the Automat.

However, if you marry, I suggest you look in other fields. In a city as big as New York I am sure there are pants manufacturers, wholesale delicatessen dealers, and various other merchants who have daughters who conceivably have virtues even more indispensable to a nearsighted major comic than a talent for high kicking.

So steer clear of these coryphées. This doesn't necessarily mean that you have to snub them.

Remember they too are people, even though they spend most of their waking hours grinding and bumping. I suggest that when you arrive at the theater give them a hearty but dignified greeting. You might even toss in a low, courtly bow. Under no circumstances shake their hands, for the slightest physical contact can lead to disaster.

If there are not too many in the group, you might inquire solicitously about their health. If you are in a particularly gracious mood, you might even give them a brief résumé of *your* physical condition. The social amenities out of the way, walk quickly to your dressing room, and unless there is a fire backstage, don't emerge until the call boy has notified you that it is time to make your entrance. Your behavior on the road we can discuss at some future date. You realize, of course, that once you get to Altoona, Sioux City, and other way stations, you may have to modify your attitude, but judging from the reviews this is a problem that need not concern you for some time.

So look smart, be smart, and remember . . . in Union there is alimony.

Love,

Groucho

This letter from Groucho to Norman Krasna further demonstrates the pungency of Groucho's wit:

June 6, 1957

Dear Mr. Krasna:

I'm sorry I couldn't come to your party the other night, but in my declining years I've become a social butterfly. Take the other evening, for example. I donned evening clothes (which took considerable preparation as the suit doesn't fit too well) and went to a very lavish, flower-bedecked party at Romanoff's. It was predicted that this would be one of the social events of the season. Even George Raft would be there. Well, to make a short party long—there were beautiful women all over the place, champagne was flowing, and I wound up with George Raft.

Regards,

Groucho

We'll leave Groucho—for the moment—with one of his most famous *bons mots*: In 1965 he wrote to the president of a Hollywood club:

Please accept my resignation. I don't care to belong to any club that will have me as a member.

## Fred Allen

FRED ALLEN was one of the funniest men of his time, and he deserves to be better remembered today than he is. By the time he died in 1956, he had been a star in vaudeville, musical comedy, movies, radio, and television. James Thurber himself once remarked, "You can count on the thumb of one hand the American who is at once a comedian, a humorist, a wit, and a satirist, and his name is Fred Allen."

Indeed, humor simply flowed from the man, almost as if he couldn't help it. Here are some excerpts from letters to various friends that showcase his spontaneous wit:

> Those mosquitoes in New Jersey are so big, one of them stung a Greyhound bus the other night and it swelled up so badly they couldn't get it into the Lincoln Tunnel.

> His hair looks like the elbow of an old raccoon coat.

> I am the only man who has cut his throat with his tongue.

> Things are so tough up here that people who have been living on the cuff are moving farther up the sleeve for the summer.

You can't go through life writing with your tongue in your cheek. Half the world will think you chew tobacco and the other half will think you have bitten off the end of somebody's goiter.

⌒

On his radio program, Allen said he once checked into a hotel in Philadelphia and the rooms were so small even the mice were humpbacked. The Philadelphia Chamber of Commerce, the Convention of Tourists Committee, and the All Philadelphia Citizens Committee all promptly sent up a howl of protest. Even *The Public Ledger* attacked him in an editorial entitled "Philadelphia Fights Back." Allen replied with a letter to the editor that made all his attackers look pretty silly:

> dr. editor,
>     the remarks made on my program concerned a small theatrical hotel in phila. twenty-five years ago. no mention was made on my program and no aspersions cast on the many excellent hotels in phila. today. i know that the benjamin franklin hotel is so named because you can fly a kite in any room. i know that the rooms at the walton are so large the world's fair is stopping there when it goes on the road next fall. i know that the rooms at the bellevur-stratford are so spacious that the army-navy game can be played in a closet. and i know that billy rose

rehearsed his aquacade in a sink in one of mr.
lamaze's mastodonic bathrooms at the warwick.

yrs., fred allen

⌒

Here's a letter Allen wrote to a book dealer and close
friend, Frank Rosengren, from Maine in 1932, where he and
his wife, Portland, annually rented a vacation house.

Dear Frank:

The normal season here in Maine for vacationists
starts on July first and ends after Labor Day. Having
nothing better to do this month, we decided to come
up ahead of the average tourist and see why nobody
comes here until July.

And now we know. We have been here at Old Or-
chard six days and it has been colder than an Eskimo
street walker's big toe on a dull night. Goose pimples
come to a head here and give off a sort of liquid frost
when pressed unduly. The people eat candles and use
the wicks for dental floss and business is so bad in fish
markets you can hear a fin drop.

We are constantly bombarded by nudists who stop
at the door begging for an old vest or a sock or any
article of clothing to tide them over the chilly period.
This morning I heard a knock and found a nudist
who is an English gentleman shivering at the front of
the house. He was wearing a monocle in his navel.

Being confined to the house, as we have been, has led to interior decoration. A new curtain has been hung on the front door so that my birthmarks and other blemishes will not be common gossip. I, who know nothing of machines, have installed a radio set with a lightning arrester and ground wire. The arrester has sort of an ego complex and seems to be looking up, daring lightning to start something. I hope that the God in charge of the Bolt Delivery Service can take a joke. Otherwise a nance clap of thunder will reduce this place to a decoy for stray dogs. I am sorry now that I wasted so much time on the radio set. All one hears is stale jokes and much ado about certain songs being sung through the special permission of the coffee-right owners. I may demolish the bothersome contraption in a moment given over to a personal decibel movement. I'll let you know later.

I have also tacked up soap dishes, coat hangers, and put some brads in a quaking chair. I say "tacked up" advisedly. We'll still only be here two months and I see no reason why I should waste energy, which I am bound to need in later life, actually nailing up fixtures. Should anything collapse, through some faux pas of a guest, one of those "Oh, I didn't know it was tacked up" incidents, I shan't feel obliged to worry about it. We are doing our best to discourage guests. My brother spent the weekend with us and left tonight ill from exposure and undernourishment. If he will only get mad enough to talk about his experience around home, we may be able to scare off any prospective cadgers and callers.

I addressed the mice, on the day of arrival. I put it to them squarely that it was up to them to look to the Maine Society for the Preservation and Culture of Rodents for sustenance. I have no intention of having a lot of those sneaky mice pimping in the kitchen. I'll keep them out if I have to go downstairs at night and mew for an hour or so before going to bed. I have put a scarecrow in front of the package of bran since learning that crows, faced with a corn shortage, have turned to puffed rice, and other breakfast foods. . . .

I hoped to write several scenes here but my aunts are coming for a rest which I need more than they do and then [wife] Portland's kid sisters are coming which means a period of bedlam and waiting to get into the bathroom. Life is futile and the man who wears a toupée should take his hat off to no one. . . .

⌒

Allen's letter to the New York Insurance Department reads like a detailed treatment for an elaborate slapstick sequence in a Buster Keaton movie:

June 18, 1932

Dear Sir:

The soullessness of corporations is something to stun you. . . . I went around last Sunday morning to a new house that is being built for me. On the top floor I found a pile of bricks which were not needed there. Feeling industrious, I decided to remove the bricks. In the elevator shaft there was a rope and a pulley, and on one end of the rope was a barrel. I pulled the barrel up to the top, after walking down the ladder, and then fastened the rope firmly at the bottom of the shaft. Then I climbed the ladder again and filled the barrel with bricks. Down the ladder I climbed again, five floors, mind you, and untied the rope to let the barrel down. The barrel was heavier than I was and before I had time to study over the proposition, I was going up the shaft with my speed increasing at every floor. I thought of letting go of the rope, but before I had decided to do so I was so high that it seemed more dangerous to let go than to hold on, so I held on.

Halfway up the elevator shaft I met the barrel of bricks coming down. The encounter was brief and spirited. I got the worst of it but continued on my way toward the roof—that is, most of me went on, but much of my epidermis clung to the barrel and returned to earth. Then I struck the roof the same time the barrel struck the cellar. The shock knocked the breath out of me and the bottom out of the barrel. Then I was heavier than the empty barrel, and I started down while the barrel started up. We went and met in the middle of our journey, and the barrel uppercut me, pounded my solar plexus, barked my shins, bruised my body, and skinned my face. When we became untangled, I resumed my downward journey and the barrel went higher. I was soon at the bottom. I stopped so suddenly that I lost my presence of mind and let go of the rope. This released the barrel which was at the top of the elevator shaft and it fell five floors and landed squarely on top of me, and it landed hard too.

Now, here is where the heartlessness . . . comes in. I sustained five accidents in two minutes. One on my way up the shaft, when I met the barrel of bricks, the second when I met the roof, the third when I was descending and I met the empty barrel, the fourth when I struck the barrel, and the fifth when the barrel struck me. But the insurance man said that it was one accident not five and instead of receiving payment for injuries at the rate of five times $25, I only get one $25 payment. I, therefore, enclose my policy and ask that you cancel the same as I made up my mind that henceforth I am not to be skinned by either barrel or/and my insurance company.

Yours sincerely and regretfully,
Fred Allen

This letter by Allen to syndicated gossip columnist Earl Wilson is practically a succession of one-liners, all in Allen's bizarre typography:

dear earl . . .

sorry I can't write a guest column for you. column writing isn't my metier. (metier is french for racket) i could never be a bistro balzac, a saloon sandburg, or a diva de maupassant.

An m.c. on a quiz program once told me that einstein knows more about space than any columnist. i told him that a columnist fills more space in a week than einstein can hope to fill in a lifetime. einstein keeps going for years with one lousy theory. to weather a day, you need two columns of facts.

and what facts! i could never take your place.

with gay abandon you write of falsies and girdles and elaborate on their contents. i blush when i see breast of chicken on a menu. the first time i saw jane russell i wondered how she got her kneecaps up in her sweater.

. . . you are welcomed at all of the fine eating places. mr. billingsly, they say, carries you over the threshold of his stork club nightly.

the last time i ate in lindy's the tongue in my

sandwich gave me the raspberry through a small hole in the top slice of bread. when i complained to lindy he put his head in the sandwich and gave me another raspberry through a small hole in the bottom slice of bread.

when you walk down broadway, you meet scores of interesting people.

when i walk down broadway I meet jack benny or some other actor who is out of work.

the nights you go into toots shor's, oscar levant, between sips of coffee, is bellowing epigrams. to wit: "i ran myself through an adding machine today and found that i didn't amount to much."

the nights i go into shor's toots is generally talking to himself in a low voice. i can't even hear what he is saying. the only time i could hear him, toots was mumbling, "why you big crum bum, you're so stupid you think yellow jack is chinese money."

when you go to an opening, noel coward stops you at intermission and regales you with the story that is currently sweeping london. to wit: the one about the young innocent girl whose father told her about the flowers but neglected to tell her about the b's. the girl went to hollywood and made three bad pictures.

the last opening i attended (life with father) a guy named dwight gristle, who was selling black market tassels, told me a broken down gag about a new cheese store—it was called "limberger heaven."

how could i ever get enough good jokes together to be "earl for a day?"

last night, i walked around town. here's what happened to me.

at the health food store, on 50th street, i saw a sign "hubert frend has switched to yogurt."

at the copa, jack eigan told me about the latest in hollywood styles: an undertaker is featuring a suede coffin.

at the automat, jack haley told me about the picture star who thought he was a banana. his psychiatrist found the picture star had a split personality. his is the first banana split personality on record.

you can see, earl, the whole thing is futile. i can never be a columnist. I know the wrong people. i hear the wrong things. i go to the wrong places.

i will end up like the old man who lived in the cannon for twenty years—he was always hoping to be a big shot, but he never quite made it.

sorry to have let you down with the guest column.

regards . . .

fred allen

In May 1945, as World War II was winding down, Allen wrote Broadway director and hit comedy writer Abe

Burrows, on the occasion of Burrows's resignation from the *Duffy's Tavern* radio program.

dear freelance . . .

we read that you had resigned from the duffy's tavern enterprises. i think you have made a smart move. like the infantry frank loesser mentions in his song about roger young, there is no glory in radio. if norman corwin had done the work he has done in radio in any other medium he would have morganthau's hand in his pocket and a standing in the theater or in hollywood that would be enviable. the excellent work you have done in radio, apart from the satisfaction you have gotten, the money you have earned, and the opportunity you have had to experiment with ideas to perfect your technique, is transient. in pictures, or in the theater, you can work less, make as much money, and acquire a reputation that will mean something. a radio writer can only hope for ulcers or a heart attack in his early forties. with few exceptions radio is a bog of mediocrity where little men with carbon minds wallow in sluice of their own making. for writers with talent and ideas, after it has served its purpose as a training ground, radio is a waste of creative time. good luck to you in new fields of endeavor, mr. b., long may you gambol!

recently a hollywood reporter mentioned that a

mr. abe burrows was cutting a social dove-wing out there and that claudette colbert wouldn't think of giving a party without a caterer and this burroughs. we assume that with this nature spelling you are attending claudette incognito. i hope you have the piano shawl in the act. if you can't get one of those shawls you might get a navajo blanket. an indian blanket with a. burrows sewed on in birchbark would attract attention before you gained the piano. i am working on a new cellophane sheet of music. this will enable the pianist to look through his music and see how people are reacting to his efforts. many times an entertainer is singing his heart out and behind his music guests are holding their noses or doing acrostics. with the cellophane music sheet the guest will know that the soloist can see him and he will act accordingly. I have another invention you may want later. this is a time stink bomb that explodes in the foyer as guests walk out on the singer. the odor drives the guests back into the room until the artist concludes his program. let me know if you are in the market for any of these parlor devices.

   yours until hitler's body is found . . .
   f. allen

now that mussolini is dead the devil at least has a straightman.

# Groucho Marx and Fred Allen

DURING THE EARLY 1950s, Groucho Marx and his friend Fred Allen had quite a wily exchange of letters, mostly revolving around their involvements in the radio and the advent of television. Like all great correspondence, these letters really take on a life of their own. Here are some priceless excerpts (note that Allen continued to make highly erratic—and characteristic—use of capitalization):

Groucho wrote, on March 20, 1950:

> I am beginning to regard myself as the kiss of death to any branch of the amusement industry. When I reached big-time vaudeville it immediately began to rot at the seams. During the days when I was a movie actor, no theater could survive unless it gave away dishes, cheese and crackers, and, during Lent, costume jewelry. I remember one midnight leaving the Marquis Theater in Hollywood after a triple feature with two pounds of Gold Meadow butter, a carton of Pepsi-Cola, and 12 chances on a soft water tank.
>
> And now I am having the same effect on radio. . . . I am now 5th in the national ratings, but who the hell is [getting polled]? I can't find anyone who admits they still have a radio, let alone listens to one. Luckily, my sponsor's employees are on strike so he has no

way of knowing whether I am selling cars or not. The rich people, or potential car buyers, are the ones who have the television sets. The paupers, or schlepper crowd, still hang on to their portable radios, but unfortunately they're not the ones who buy Chryslers and De Soto station wagons. So my guess is that as soon as the strike is settled, the Chrysler Corp. will ask me to move over to television. Little do they know that in a few short months I will have this new medium croaking its death rattle.

Fred Allen's reply, in part:

i do not think you are the asp that has bestowed the kiss of death on vaudeville, the picture industry and radio. vaudeville committed suicide, the picture business ran out of adjectives and radio was thrown to the cretin. at the present time, your radio show is the only one that is mentioned by critics and listeners who, because they have dirty windows and cannot see the aerials of their neighbors' roofs, do not know about television and still listen to radio. if you want to give television the buss of rigor mortis you had better hurry. after a few recent shows, dogs in this section have been dragging television sets out into the yards and burying them.

In May 1951, Groucho wrote to Fred, taking more than a few hilarious jabs at the Easterner's perception of California as a backwater:

> I was just about to answer your letter when word was flashed through Southern California that you were soon to arrive for one more assault against the motion picture industry, this time with Ginger Rogers. Well, if you have to go that's the way to go.
>
> If you do come alone be sure to bring some fishing tackle, for my cellar leaks, and we can have a high old time down there, swapping stories and exchanging worms.
>
> . . . The May wine is just beginning to acquire its full body. You see, because of the difference in time, the wine you drink in the east early in the spring only comes into its full maturity here during the winter solstice. And the crops have been beautiful. The Lord, Fred, has been mighty good to us. We harvested enough corn not only for us, but for the [live]stock as well, and the syrup has been flowing as though it were possessed. Mother says I am blasphemous, but we all have to have our little joke. We look for a hard winter, for only yesterday I noticed an extra growth of fur on the left side of my upstairs maid, and that means the storms will soon be upon us.
>
> Other than this there is nothing to tell you. As you

know, we miss the clump of your hobnailed boots on our eiderdown, and can only hope and pray that ere long Ethan Allen will give up that silly siege of Fort Ticonderoga and send you back to us. Well, I'm fagged out now so I guess I'll turn in. Last night I spent almost the whole night shucking corn and mother says I'm not shuckin' as well as I used to. I guess I must be getting on. Mother also said I'm not getting on as often as I used to. Well, that's the way it goes.

Love,

Groucho

P.S. The brood sow is with pig again.

Later that year, Fred wrote to Groucho, chiding him for the irregularity of his correspondence:

Dear Groucho:

i know that you must derive much more pleasure dashing off a note to some old bag you hope to tree on your next trip east than you do writing to . . . me. there is an old legend written on the wall of the men's room at the martha washington hotel. it reads—it is better to marry a young girl and satisfy her curiosity than to marry a widow and disappoint her. . . .

Groucho retorted:

Despite the fact that I regard myself as an extremely glamorous figure, I rarely receive any mail that would indicate that the fair sex, as a sex, has any interest in me. No cravats, no Johnson & Murphy shoes, no expensive stogies ever darken my mailbox. The following is a brief sampling of what nestles in my wastebasket this morning.

The first envelope I opened was from a quack cruising under the pseudonym of Dr. Bendricks. Apparently he has seen me on TV, for he wrote that he could equip me with a new set of atomic glands. He calls his method the "Chemistry of Natural Immunity." He said he was confident that these new glands would do the trick. I am not sure what trick he was referring to but it certainly sounded encouraging. Unfortunately, I have no idea who Bendricks is. Is he a reputable scientist? The whole thing is too much for me. . . .

The next letter was from the proprietor of a Beverly Hills liquor store, and a gloomier prophet I have rarely read. He warned me that liquor prices were going sky high and that I had better lay away 30 or 40 cases of hard booze before war is officially declared. Since my drinking these days is confined to swallowing a thimbleful of cooking sherry each night before dinner, his letter left me in a fairly calm condition.

The third letter was from the Continental Can

Company, pleading with me to spend my proxy on my 100 shares of stock which, incidentally, have gone down seven points since I bought them. The letter pointed out, rather querulously I thought, that I was a stockholder in a giant and growing corporation, but that its officers were helpless to proceed with the business at hand unless I was willing to cooperate and send in my proxy, and pronto. The whole company, they implied, was going to hell. Thousands of stockholders were sitting in a drafty auditorium in Wilmington, Delaware, unable to unseat the present officials unless they were morally strengthened by my proxy.

The next letter was from the Electric Bond and Share Company (in case you've forgotten, this is the uptown equivalent of Goldman-Sachs). In 1929 this outfit reduced my bank account by $38,000. Unfortunately, through some confusion in the bookkeeping department, I find myself 21 years later, still the owner of one-half share. In case you are not too familiar with current Wall Street prices, an entire share can be purchased for $1.10. They, too, were after my proxy. I have tried many times to dispose of this shrunken security. One year in desperation I even sent them the half share, special delivery and registered, but a few days later it came back—this time to make matters worse, with six cents postage due. One year I destroyed the God-damned stock, but it didn't faze EB&S one bit. I am on their books and apparently they are determined to keep me there—at least until the next market crash.

The next was a letter from AFRA. They pointed out that I was some months behind in my dues and unless the money was forthcoming in the near future they were planning on pulling out the musicians, stage hands, cameramen, electricians, studio policemen, and an ex-vice president of radio who stands in front of NBC giving away free ducats for Spade Cooley.

So, Fred, I say to hell with the U.S. mails. I would be deeply indebted to you if you would write your congressman asking him to vote against any further appropriations for the post office. Without funds this monster would soon wither away and die and I could then spend my declining years with an empty wastebasket and a light heart.

Fred's reply came several weeks later:

dear groucho—

your recent letter, complaining about the quality of fan mail you have been receiving, has had to await a reply until your problem had been thoroughly mulled. unlike cider mulling, this takes time. the man bent on mulling a batch of cider merely heats his poker, or his shish kebab lance, over an open fire and plunges it into his cider. a man who mulls over a letter may be busy mulling for weeks.

it seems to me that your dilemma is posed by high standards. you cater to a class of radio and tv owner who can write. when you appeal to a literate element, people who not only own radio and tv sets but who also own pens and pencils and know how to use them, you have to expect mail.

if you are going to eliminate mail you cannot hope to do it through closing up the post office and the postal department. without the post office politicians would have no places to put their brothers-in-law. you can only stop this avalanche of fan mail through lowering your standards and going after the illiterate crowd.

# Hermione Gingold

ACTRESS HERMIONE GINGOLD once got a nasty letter complaining that her performance in *Fallen Angel* was "a disgusting exhibition" and "a slur on English womanhood." Oddly, the letter was signed "A Friend." Gingold's reply appeared in her book *Sirens Should Be Seen and Not Heard*:

Dear Friend,

How clever and capricious you are, cloaking yourself in anonymity, and I must confess I cannot for the life of me guess which of my many friends you can be. You have sent my head spinning and my imagination whirling. Could you be found among my dear friends, intimate friends, close friends, childhood friends, pen friends, family friends, friends of a friend, friends in distress, friends who are closer than a brother, friends in need, or school friends? Your letter quite clearly shows that you are not illiterate, and therefore we can rule out my school friends. Your masterly command of the language banishes the thought that you could be found among my friends from overseas. Your witty criticism of my performance makes me think that I might find you amongst my nearest and dearest "bosom friends," that is, if you did not choose to address me as "Dear Madam"—a clever move this, and one that reduces my last thought to mere stupidity and you to a "casual acquaintance."

An awful thought has dawned—it is all a joke—and you aren't really my friend at all. I must try to dismiss this thought. It depresses me. To lose a friend like you in a few words, oh no.

So, dear anonymous friend, if this should chance to meet your eye, please keep your promise and come round one night—yes, and bring your friends, too, for I know intuitively that your friends will be my friends.

Cordially yours,
Hermione Gingold

# Bob Hope

DURING THE FILMING of *Fancy Pants*, Bob Hope was thrown from a prop horse. Although he wasn't seriously injured, he underwent a series of complicated medical examinations and tests. Afterward, he wrote the following letter to Paramount head Henry Ginsburg:

Dear Henry:

I want to thank you for your kindness during my recent illness and tell you that you did not have to do it, I wasn't going to sue. . . . Inasmuch as you are going to have to explain my $4,500 doctor bills at the next stockholders' meeting (assuming you are still with the company), I think I should explain that they are not out of line.

You and I know that in the old days when a man fell on his back, he got up, tightened his belt, and walked back into the bar. . . . But medicine has made great strides during our generation. When I woke up in the hospital, four nurses were standing over me, a doctor was feeling my pulse, and a specialist was busy on the phone checking with the bank to see how much we would go for.

Then they started the tests which you find on Page Three of the bill. . . . Meantime, no one would tell me how I was doing. Finally I picked up the phone, got an outside wire, called the hospital, and asked how Bob Hope was doing. I'd taken a turn for the worse. . . . We've sure come a long ways from sulphur and molasses.

B.H.

# Eddie Cantor and Florenz Ziegfeld

THE LEGENDARY SHOWMAN Florenz Ziegfeld was well known for his constant and frantic use of the telephone and telegram. He would often send his performers telegrams after watching their work from the back of the theater, offering criticisms or suggestions. Once, when Eddie Cantor was playing *Kid Boots* in Chicago, he received a twelve-page telegram from Ziegfeld with a variety of suggestions, from line changes to the removal of an entire song, and remarks about the other performers, certain scenes that needed attention, and so forth. The entire telegram was such a jumble of questions, Cantor knew that to address each question would result in the longest telegraphed interchange ever conducted. So he simply wired back:

Yes.

This did nothing to deter Ziegfeld, who promptly fired off another telegram, twice as long as the previous missive, which ended:

What do you mean, Yes? Do you mean yes you will take out the song, or yes you will put in the lines, or yes you will fix that scene? Or yes you have talked to the other actors?

Cantor wired back:

No.

# Andy Rooney

ANDY ROONEY could be called the greatest curmudgeon of our time. And even at his crankiest, he can be riotously funny.

He's justly famous for being able to summon strong—and often contrary—opinions about practically everything on the planet. Here, in a letter to a Ms. Worth, he gives it to poetry—but good!

Dear Ms. Worth,

Thank you for your invitation to the poetry reading next Tuesday evening at the YMCA, by what you call "three outstanding local versifiers."

I don't understand most poems when they're printed, even after I've read them over several times. If I don't understand a poem in print, how could I understand a poem that's read aloud just once, and often poorly, by its author?

I don't like to sound like a know-nothing but it is my opinion that most of the people who like to call themselves poets are no more poets than all the people who paint pictures are artists.

I don't know when poets decided the end of one line doesn't have to rhyme with the end of the next one—or, at the very least, the one after that. To me, if it doesn't rhyme, it isn't poetry. Robert Frost said;

"Writing free verse is like playing tennis with the net down."

Carl Sandburg, whose work I often confuse with Robert Frost's, said "poetry is a spot halfway between where you listen and where you wonder what it was you heard."

I still read some poetry in *Harper's, The Atlantic*, and *The New Yorker* just to make sure I still don't like it. I don't know whether it's my lack of taste or lack of intellect that fails to attract me to modern poetry. I'm careful to say "modern" because there are hundreds of old poems and books of poetry that I like and reread. Most of what I like rhymes. Modern poets feel superior to poets, new and old, whose verses rhyme. They are brothers-in-art to the painters who don't feel that what they put on canvas has to be OF anything. All of it, the paint and the poetry has so much hidden meaning that it hurts my teeth to think of.

Some newspapers print poems regularly. They are often either unintelligible or just plain bad. I'd like to meet an editor who chooses the poetry and ask him a few questions.

"Am I not a person of average intelligence who should be able to comprehend a poem?"
"Why don't I?"
"Am I culturally retarded?"

"Heaven forbid and I hardly dare mention it but
. . . are you sure it isn't the poet's fault?"
"Is there any possibility that the poet conned you,
the editor, into thinking there was more content
to his words than is apparent to me from reading
them?"

When I was in high school, I could get all choked
up reading Edna St. Vincent Millay. In her later years
she wrote about getting old.

> "I only know that summer sang in me
> A little while, that in me sings no more."

Pardon me for saying so, Edna, but now that I'm
old it strikes me as pretentious hot air. Life—
summer, winter, fall, or spring—sings in me as it
always did and I don't want the music to stop.

I'll tell you why I think poets write lines whose
meaning isn't clear. I think that they don't have a
clear idea themselves of what it is they're trying to
say. I further think that if they did have a clear idea
and wrote it down clearly as prose, it wouldn't
amount to much.

Tell me I'm wrong but explain clearly why. Poets
themselves have always been defensive about poetry.
In college I read Shelley's "A Defence of Poetry."
Shelley was a poet I understood and I wonder if he'd
defend the modern poets?

Maybe you could make the readings by the three

poets more interesting next week to people who don't care much for poetry, by making a contest out of it. Give two prizes—one to the poet who reads best and another to the one whose poems are judged to be the best. A crass contest like that might bring the poets back down to earth.

Here Rooney turns his curmudgeonly attention to "celebrity cookbooks." His own explanatory headnote precedes the letter:

Anyone whose name is known to more than ten people gets frequent requests from people assembling what they call "a celebrity cookbook." Years ago I got one from a columnist for the *New York Times*, Enid Nemy, whose work I had read and admired. She said she was putting together a book of favorite potato recipes of well-known people and would like a contribution from me.

In a moment of pique, I put down an outrageously impractical recipe for "Baked Potato Ice Cream" and sent it to her with a note:

Dear Enid,

When dinner is over and I disappear into the kitchen my guests invariably start chatting incoherently in anxious anticipation of what I've prepared for dessert. (Do I have the genre so far?)

Although I hesitate to select one potato recipe as my best I must say that I get a great many favorable comments on my potato ice cream. Don't serve this to guests who are calorie conscious.

Take four large Idaho potatoes. Peel them, setting the peels aside. Cut the potatoes longwise into half-inch slices. Discard the rounded top and bottom slices. Place the stack of slices, which now have a flat surface, on the cutting board and slice them again, producing long fingers of potato. Turn these parallel to the edge of the cutting board and slice them once more into small cubes.

In six cups of water, to which you have added a cup and a quarter of sugar, simmer the potato cubes until the water evaporates and one of the cubes adheres to a single chopstick. Place cooked potatoes in blender with two cups of heavy cream and a dash of paprika for color and blend until well . . . blended. My mother, who taught me how to make this, used to serve it to us as a treat when we were good.

Pour the potato mixture into a divided ice cube tray and place in freezer. If you have a microwave freezer, all the better. When mixture begins to thicken, but before it hardens, insert one toothpick in each and continue freezing. Mixtures should be of such consistency that the toothpick stands upright. When toothpick no longer pulls out easily or turns blue, the potato ice cream cubes are ready. Plan on three cubes per guest and serve with a bowl of rich chocolate sauce for dipping.

After dinner, throw out the potato peels.

Imagine Rooney's sheer incredulity when Nemy's editor called him six weeks later to ask him in all seriousness how many people this preposterous recipe would serve. The publisher included the recipe in Nemy's book, and when Nemy found out the recipe was a parody, she was so furious that she stopped speaking to Rooney.

A woman named Susan Parris, assembling her own celebrity cookbook to benefit her son's school, heard about the potato ice cream fiasco and chastised Rooney in a letter. His reply:

Mrs. Susan Connolly Parris
Trenton, New Jersey
Dear Mrs. Parris,

There's a great deal of idiocy about celebrity in America and I have no desire to contribute to it. Enid Nemy is a big girl now and if she undertook to collect a cookbook she should, at the very least, have known enough about food to recognize a joke when she read one.

I don't think any responsible publisher would issue a cookbook without having kitchen-tested the recipes.

There are two possibilities:

1.  They tested my recipe for Baked Potato Ice
    Cream and found it to be delicious.
2.  They knew it was a joke and thought it
    would be fun to have in a book that no one
    would take seriously anyway.

As for your own celebrity cookbook, making an
effort may relieve a helpless feeling you have but I
suspect the proceeds will amount to less than [what]
a few well-directed requests from rich friends would
net for your son's school.

Sorry we disagree. It's my opinion celebrity
cookbooks are nonsense and should be treated as
such.

⌣

As you'd expect, Andy Rooney is inundated with letters
from people who have ideas for his *60 Minutes* segments.
Here's his reply to one such letter, from a Jacqueline Arm-
strong:

Dear Jacqueline,

When someone sends in an idea, I don't often
respond because the idea is either terrible, I've
already done it, or they sue if I use it. Several years
ago, I was coming up to my office in the elevator on
a rainy day. Everyone was dripping and one young
woman said, "You ought to do a piece on umbrellas."

I did a piece on umbrellas and that's the last time I recall taking a suggestion from anyone. (The basic problem with umbrellas is, the handle is right in the middle of where you want to stand to stay dry.)

All that stuff of yours is good but it's a written piece, not for television. Years ago I did an hour for Harry Reasoner called "The Strange Case of the English Language." It was fun for me and reasonably successful but the number of people who care about the niceties of usage don't make a large television audience.

Two weeks ago I took a piece to Hewitt on the subject of the ways we write our alphabet. Handwritten letters are hard to read because there are too many different ways to form our letters. The small "r" is easily mistaken for an "n." Capital "D" or capital "R" are ridiculous letters when written with all the flourishes so many people use. Don hated the idea.

For years, when I write letters, I've dropped the apostrophes from words that are unmistakeable without them but I can't get a publisher to go along with it in a book. "Dont," "isnt," "arent," "wont," "wasnt." It's hard to be consistent though because you need the apostrophe in "she's," "we're," etc.

While there isn't usually as much excuse for writing excess verbiage in a written piece, some fat is understandable and even necessary in spoken English. We all speak faster than people can listen and there has to be some padding in the language to give people time to hear—and ourselves time to get the next thought ready before we say it. Clichés are useful for that purpose, too.

But thanks. I really did like your ideas.

Sincerely,

Andy Rooney

Rooney really had the last say on why one wouldn't want to give out autographs. Every night, he throws away eight to ten self-addressed stamped envelopes from people who want an autographed photograph. He wrote an amusing and characteristically rankled letter to an Eleanor Mahoney to explain why:

Dear Eleanor Mahoney,

This is in response to your letter asking for my autograph. I don't sign my name on a sheet of paper for people who ask me to do that and for some reason, your letter has moved me to try to say why.

If you're going to succeed, you have to have confidence in yourself and it's difficult to be confident without being too confident. It amuses me to think that my appraisal of myself is close to what it ought to be. I'm not egotistical but I'm not especially modest.

It's best if you can count out what other people

say they think of you. Everyone wants people to like them and, generally speaking, we all try to make friends with everyone we meet. We hope they overestimate us. We don't want them to have an accurate opinion of us. We want them to have a better opinion of us than we deserve. That's why we smile even though nothing strikes us as funny and we praise them even if they haven't done much to deserve it. We tell stories about ourselves that make us look good and skip the ones that make us look bad.

All that may be okay but if we succeed in making people think more highly of us than we deserve, it's best if we, at least, don't take their elevated opinion of us seriously.

I'm recognizable to a lot of people and they write me for my autograph, as you have, because of my regular appearance on television.

I hope you'll excuse me for saying that people everywhere, but Americans in particular, have this dumb way of equating celebrity with excellence, competence, and intelligence in everything.

Those attributes don't have much to do with being well known. The well-known person usually knows how to do one thing well but he or she is not necessarily a wonderful or exceptionally smart person because of it.

I've almost certainly given a lot of people the

impression I'm a conceited jerk because I won't write my name on the card or piece of paper that they push at me on the street or in a restaurant.

I was thinking I ought to be clear in my own mind why I won't give my autograph. To begin with, if it's important to make an accurate appraisal of yourself, it's certainly best if you make that appraisal without any help from outside. You shouldn't put much faith in what other people think of your ability—and that goes both ways, too. You shouldn't get thinking you're better than you are because other people think you're good and you shouldn't get depressed when other people have a low opinion of your ability. You ought to decide for yourself.

Just as soon as I write my name on a piece of paper, I'm agreeing with the person who asks for it that I'm a wonderful person whose autograph is worth saving. This is nonsense and I refuse to be put in that embarrassing position. When you ask me for my autograph you are demeaning yourself and forcing more esteem on me than I'm worth.

At least I'm going to use your stamped envelope to send you this letter instead of throwing it away.

Sincerely,

Andy Rooney

# Aaron Copland

THE BOSTON PREMIERE of Aaron Copland's rather challenging Piano Concerto was held in 1927, with Copland himself at the piano and Serge Koussevitzky conducting the Boston Symphony Orchestra. Following the premiere, numerous audience members forwarded their splenetic reactions to the Boston newspapers. These letters were sent to Copland by his friend Nicolas Slonimsky. Copland replied to Slonimsky with the following gleefully sarcastic letter:

> Dear Kolya,
>
> You're a darling to have sent all those delightful write-ups. After reading them I went to the mirror to see if I could recognize myself.
>
> How flattering it was to read that the "Listener" can understand Strauss, Debussy, Stravinsky—but not poor me. How instructive to learn that there is "no rhythm in this so-called concerto." And how badly I felt for Mrs. Gardner of Bridgeport when I thought how badly *she* must have felt when she discovered her mistake in the title. Only one thing got my nanny—how dare H.T.P. talk of *reducing* me to my level, when I am waiting to be *raised* to my level. And all that really worries me is whether or not the Maestro will ever again have sufficient courage to perform me anywhere. . . .

When the Concerto is played again ("O horrid thought!") we must see if we can't get the police to raid the concert hall to give a little added interest to this "horrible" experiment.

Till soon,

Aaron Copland

# *Julia Child*

FROM TIME TO TIME throughout her illustrious career, Julia Child was attacked by people she began to refer to as "food police"—those who thought her recipes and culinary edicts were too high-fat and unhealthy. One such attacker wrote asking why Child couldn't advocate healthy foods in her books and television programs—after all, she'd been seen in public eating a salad.

Julia sent her the following recipe for a healthy life:

> Small helpings,
> no seconds,
> eat a little bit of everything,
> no snacking,
> have a good time,
> and pick your grandparents!

# PERMISSION ACKNOWLEDGMENTS

QUENTIN CRISP

Permission to quote Quentin Crisp's letter dated 10/23/1980 to Denise is granted by Stedman Mays and Mary Tahan of Clausen, Mays & Tahan Literary Agency, LLC. All rights reserved.

ANDY ROONEY

From *Sincerely, Andy Rooney* by Andy Rooney. Copyright © 1999 by Andy Rooney. Reprinted with permission of Perseus Books, L.L.C.

HERMIONE GRINGOLD

From *Funny Letters from Famous People* edited by Bill Adler. Copyright © 1969 by Bill Adler. Reprinted with permission of Scholastic, Inc.

BOB HOPE

From *Funny Letters from Famous People* edited by Bill Adler. Copyright © 1969 by Bill Adler. Reprinted with permission of Scholastic, Inc.

AARON COPLAND

From *Funny Letters from Famous People* edited by Bill Adler. Copyright © 1969 by Bill Adler. Reprinted with permission of Scholastic, Inc.

# ABOUT THE AUTHOR

Charles Osgood has been anchor of *CBS News Sunday Morning* since 1994. He also anchors and writes *The Osgood File*, his daily news commentary broadcast on the CBS Radio Network.

Osgood joined the ranks of the National Association of Broadcasters Hall of Fame in 1990 and was inducted into the *Broadcasting & Cable* Hall of Fame in 2000. He has received some of the highest accolades in broadcast journalism, including a 1999 International Radio & Television Society Foundation (IRTS) Award for significant achievement.

Osgood received a 1997 George Foster Peabody Award for *Sunday Morning* and two additional Peabody Awards in 1985 and 1986 for *Newsmark*, a weekly CBS Radio public affairs broadcast. He received his third Emmy Award in 1997.

Osgood edited *Kilroy Was Here* and is the author of *Nothing Could Be Finer Than a Crisis That Is Minor in the Morning, There's Nothing That I Wouldn't Do If You Would Be My POSSLQ, Osgood on Speaking: How to Think on Your Feet Without Falling on Your Face, The Osgood Files*, and *See You on the Radio*.

He lives in New York City with his wife, Jean. They have five children.